Kristine McGuire w .... ability as she shares her experiences as a witch, medium, and ghost hunter. Without sensationalism or glorification of evil, Kristine effectively walks the reader through personal and sometimes terrifying experiences and into the beautiful deliverance. Using Scripture to anchor her words, she encourages the church to love and not condemn those trapped in Satan's snare. A must-read for Christian parents.

—TRACEY BATEMAN
Author of *Widow of Saunders Creek*

Confronting the growing pop culture interest in the paranormal and taking the reader through the many stages of her initial interest and subsequent professional experiences, Kristine McGuire boldly proclaims the gospel of Jesus Christ.

—KEIKI HENDRIX
The Vessel Project and Christian Book Examiner

I believe Christians need to read this book. Christians today are filled with warm fuzzies and have this adroitness to either ignore the fact there is a devil or to completely disbelieve our battle is not with flesh and blood but against the dark principalities.

—GINA BURGESS
Upon Reflection (blog)

Kristine McGuire educates readers about the dangers of the occult, while maintaining a focus on the deliverer—Jesus Christ. She does a masterful job of walking that fine line between giving too much credence to the powers of darkness and not giving enough.

—BRENDA KING
Positively Feminine (blog)

Escaping the Cauldron is a clarion call to the Christian church to confront these issues and not ignore the need for knowledge and grace-filled intervention. Kristine McGuire boldly proclaims the truth in this eye-opening, challenging, and desperately needed book in the twenty-first century.

—IBELISSE SANCHEZ-SANDERS
A Writer's Ink Horn (blog)

In *Escaping the Cauldron* Kristine McGuire reveals to us her past as a Christian witch, medium, and ghost hunter. It is a personal testimony that is powerful and informative.

—NIKOLE HAHN
Nikole Hahn's Journal (blog)

Escaping the Cauldron is engaging and informative. It should be read by anyone who is interested in the topic of the paranormal and supernatural. I encourage Christians to read it and learn from Kristine's experiences.

—BECKY WHITMORE
Associated Content (blog)

With the rise of interest in the paranormal, mediums, witchcraft, and Wicca, *Escaping the Cauldron* is incredibly helpful at sorting out the truth. Kristine McGuire's account is compelling and will open your eyes to how real the spirit realm is, first from her perspective as a witch and now her perspective as a Christian. Kristine's struggle between Christianity and witchcraft, trying to "mix" the two, will resonate in the hearts of many seekers.

—SUE CRAMER
Praise and Coffee Women's Ministries

Kristine McGuire has a unique testimony that keeps people engaged into the heart of her message. Her stories of involvement in the occult and her conclusion of how God rescued her from these traps answers many of the questions that people often have but are afraid to ask when dealing with the supernatural.

—SCOTT EIKENBERRY
Unity X-Change Seminar Coordinator

Kristine McGuire's testimony is a wake-up call to be aware of the continual influence of our culture to push us into consideration of the paranormal and other strange spiritual activity. It is also a pointed reminder that we, the church, need to be on the offensive, knowing what we believe and willing to share it with searching, hungry souls.

—RICK OPPENHUIZEN
Pastor, Grace Reformed Church

ESCAPING *the* CAULDRON

ESCAPING *the* CAULDRON

KRISTINE McGUIRE

CHARISMA
HOUSE

Cover design by Rachel Lopez
Design Director: Bill Johnson

Visit the author's website at www.kristinemcguire.com.

Library of Congress Cataloging-in-Publication Data:

McGuire, Kristine.
Escaping the cauldron / Kristine McGuire.
    p. cm.
Includes bibliographical references (p.   ).
ISBN 978-1-61638-697-9 (trade paper) -- ISBN 978-1-62136-041-4
(e-book)
1. Occultism--Religious aspects--Christianity. 2. Witchcraft. 3.
Parapsychology--Religious aspects--Christianity. I. Title.
BR115.O3M39 2012
261.5'13--dc23
                            2012018855

While the author has made every effort to provide accurate telephone
numbers and Internet addresses at the time of publication, neither the
publisher nor the author assumes any responsibility for errors or for
changes that occur after publication.

First edition

12 13 14 15 16 — 9 8 7 6 5 4 3 2 1
Printed in the United States of America

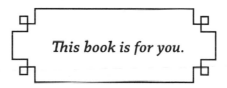

This book is for you.

CAULDRON

A large, wide-mouth metal kettle/pot; a symbol of
rebirth in witchcraft and Wicca; the womb of the
goddess.

Your eye is a lamp that provides light for your body. When your eye is good, your whole body is filled with light. But when your eye is bad, your whole body is filled with darkness. And if the light you think you have is actually darkness, how deep that darkness is!

< MATTHEW 6:22–23, NLT >

CONTENTS

Acknowledgments xvii

Introduction: What People Seek xxi

Part 1: The Occult, Wicca, and Witchcraft

1   The Occult 1

2   What Is Witchcraft? 7

3   Meeting the Goddess 12

4   The Christian Witch 22

5   Creator or Creation? 30

6   Magick: Not Prayer With Props 34

7   Eastern Meditation: Gateway to the Occult 40

8   Divination and Familiar Spirits 45

9   Prodigals Can Always Come Home 52

Part 2: Ghosts, Mediums, and the Paranormal

10   Pursuing the Paranormal 59

11   Spirits: Angels and Demons 65

12   Origins of a Ghost Hunter 70

13   Dangerous Games 80

14   Ghost Stories 84

15   Mediums and Psychics 88

16   Spirit Guides 95

17   When Demons Scream 101

18   Deliver Me From Evil 108

Part 3: Where Do We Go From Here?

19   Give Me a Spotter's Guide! 117

20   How Should Christians Respond? 120

21   Spiritual Gifts 126

22   The Dangers of Dabbling 134

23 What About Harry Potter?........................ 138

24 The Twilight Saga............................... 142

25 Scary Movies.................................. 147

26 The Origins of Halloween........................ 153

27 Spiritual Warfare............................... 160

Part 4: The Extra-Special Stuff

28 You Can Know Jesus—Ask Me How 169

29 What to Do About Yoga? 174

30 Time for the Q and A 177

Appendix A: A Glossary of Occult Words 185

Appendix B: My Ghost-Hunting Days 202

Appendix C: My 2009 Mission Trip to Costa Rica 205

Appendix D: A Note From Kristine 209

Notes 210

ACKNOWLEDGMENTS

*A*FTER REDEDICATING MY life to Christ in 2007, I was reluctant to share my testimony. God had a different plan. I saw people struggling with their faith. I heard the longing in their voices for a deeper connection with God. I saw the influence of the occult in popular culture and the subtle influence of mysticism within the church. The Holy Spirit compelled me to respond.

In August 2009 I began writing a daily blog called *Kristine ReMixed*. I included a section devoted to Christians and the Occult. By October people began e-mailing me with questions or requests for help. As I answered e-mails, counseled people over the phone, and addressed issues on my blog, I asked God, "What more should I do?" His answer was *Escaping the Cauldron*.

In this book I've shared my life with you—the good, the bad, and the strange. My prayer is that God will be honored within these pages and every person reading will find something useful to tuck away in their memory for future examination.

Books are not written without support. Please allow me to offer my heartfelt gratitude to the people who have walked through this process with me. I couldn't have done this without you!

Special thanks to:

Thom McGuire—I love you this much. That's a lot. You better believe it!

Alanna and Kari McGuire—you are the best daughters God has ever blessed a mother with. I love you.

Nancy Geertman and Karen Bartholomew, Mom and Sis—you prayed all those long years. He listened.

Ken and David B, Mark, Eric David, Shelby, Carson, Bill, Beth, Gary, and all of my family—I love you all.

Karen McGuire—thank you for encouraging me to step out in faith and write.

Ruth Kaechle—God called you as a prayer warrior. Thank you for lifting Thom and me up to the Lord over the past twenty-four years. I'm humbled.

Jeff Harshbarger (*Dancing With the Devil*, Charisma House 2012)—thank you for introducing me to the right person.

Rebeca Seitz of Glass Road Media Management—thank you for believing in me.

Jessica Dotta—you taught me to be a better writer. Lady Jane salutes you!

Barbara Dycus, Ann Mulchan, Debbie Marrie, Adrienne Gaines, Deborah Moss, Woodley August, and everyone at Charisma House—I'm so happy to be working with you all.

People who have helped share my story through blogs, interviews, and speaking events:
Kary Oberbrunner
Keiki Hendrix
Brenda King
Gina Burgess
Ibelisse Sanchez-Sanders
Nikole Hahn
Ed and Mona Weske
Mary Hess
Rick Oppenhuizen (Grace Reformed Church)
Karen Power (Christian Speaker Services)
J. R. Pittman (Ignite Radio)

Sue Cramer (Praise and Coffee)
Scott Eikenberry (Unity Christian Music Festival)
Wayne Sutton (Straight Talk With Wayne Sutton)
Lucy Ann Moll (The Sisterhood of Beautiful Warriors)
Rod Thomas (The 700 Club)
Karen Waldhart (Women's Ministry, Resurrection Life Church)
Duane Vander Klok and Joe Tucker (Resurrection Life Church)
...and so many others

Most of all:

My God...for saving me.

Introduction

WHAT PEOPLE SEEK

UMANS ARE CREATED with an inner desire for *connection*. We need to belong to someone or something outside of ourselves. Because of this we look to each other and our surroundings to find a way to be *known*. We long for our lives to have purpose beyond eating, drinking, sleeping, working, and playing before the inevitable end.

This desire drives us to find God.

I was six years old when I first understood Jesus loved me and wanted to be my Savior. I was at vacation Bible school. I don't know if I understood the deeper concept of sin, but the idea of Jesus being my friend sounded good to me, so at the end of the lesson I raised my hand. The teacher led me in a prayer asking Jesus into my heart.

Some people question whether I experienced true salvation that day. I can honestly say I was saved, and I still consider it the moment I accepted Christ. I loved God and enjoyed learning about Him. Did I ever question my salvation? Sure. I think many people do, even adults with relatively trouble-free lives. Part of my testimony is that even as a witch, God loved and protected me. So the one thing I am certain of as I look back:

I was truly saved that day.

Yet even then another darker interest crowded my thoughts—the supernatural. I was fascinated with anything spooky, scary, mystical, or just plain weird (could explain why I got picked on in elementary and junior high school, I suppose). If there was a movie on television about witches or ghosts, I watched it. When asked what I wanted to be when I grew up, my answer was, "A Gypsy fortune-teller!" Gazing into a crystal ball and predicting the future sounded cool. I wanted to know things that other people didn't know. I wanted to see the unseen, because I already sensed its presence.

As a teenager, however, I grew serious about my relationship with God. Around my sixteenth birthday I recommitted my life to Christ and began reading the Bible. I'm sure you can imagine how I felt as I discovered the things I'd dabbled in since childhood ran contrary to God's will. Thereafter I tried to avoid anything that might be construed as divination, the paranormal, or witchcraft. I ignored the daily horoscope in my teen girl magazines, which until then I'd read faithfully and applied when making decisions. Yet my interest in the occult was never truly discarded but merely stashed away—hidden, creating inner tension that continued for years.

As an adult I continued to devote myself to God. In 1988 I married a Christian man I met in college and became active in church. Having a family history of divorce, I made it my mission to have a successful Christian marriage—no matter what. So over the next few years (and by misapplying Matthew 5:48, ESV: "You therefore must be perfect, as your heavenly Father is perfect"), I pursued purity as a means of having a deeper connection with God. Conversely I believed it would help my marriage last.

The life I created became narrow-minded and legalistic. I did everything to make my relationship with my husband fit the mold of what I thought was Christian perfection. I held him to an impossibly high standard. When I had children, I was determined to raise perfect little Christians, shielding them from the world.

I lost a vital part of my understanding about God—His grace. I lost sight of the merciful nature of my Savior.

Neither my family nor I could live up to the perfection I

demanded, and I became depressed. When trouble entered our marriage, my prayers seemed unheard because I no longer felt *connected* to God. Frustrated, I looked elsewhere for spiritual relief.

In 1995, when our children were still small, my husband's job required we move to Atlanta and that he be gone five days a week. Basically I was left with the kids all day, every day. I reached a point where I needed to get out of the house or lose my mind. Therefore once a week I'd pack my little girls into a stroller and walk to the library.

As an inner debate about God and my faith grumbled in my thoughts, I scoured the religion section of the library, searching for the answers I desperately needed. I thumbed through books on ancient philosophy and various world religions, but nothing fit.

Eventually I happened upon a book about the modern revival of European goddess worship—an earth (or nature-based) religion, incorporating ancient myth, ritual, and magick, known as Wicca.

What I read appealed to my dormant interest in the occult. Everything in it, however, was contrary to what I'd been raised to believe.

I spent a week reading the book and trying the basic exercises. What surprised me was the immediate sense of welcome I received from the goddess. In fact, by the time my husband came home, I was giddy to share my discovery with him.

His reaction was less than serene.

I returned the book and focused on what had become a stale Christian existence. I buried desires for the mystical—and Wicca—deep within me, stung by guilt.

Several years passed, and guilt became anger. Bitterness grew as I tried to be a *good* Christian. My husband and I struggled emotionally and financially, and life spiraled out of control. I stopped reading the Bible and gave up on prayer altogether. Going to church became a rote exercise.

One day in late 1999, after learning my husband was also going through a crisis of faith, I decided Christianity wasn't working for me any longer. I could never be *perfect*. So finally, after twenty-nine years as a Christian, I turned my back on the church and God. I still attended services on Sunday with my family to keep up appearances, but my mind and spirit were occupied elsewhere.

Most days my husband wasn't home. He'd work late or attend some music event. We weren't talking much, leaving me to follow my secret pursuits.

Shortly after the dawn of the twenty-first century I made the final choice and committed myself to worshipping the goddess with a private ritual in my bedroom. My two young daughters slept across the hall as I lit five white candles, representing the elements of air, earth, fire, water, and spirit. I spoke an invocation, inviting the goddess to join me.

I plunged into the cauldron.

Giving into worldly temptations can provide what seems like relief, answer questions, and leave us faced with a choice. Do we stay on the path of our own desires or learn to know God on His terms?

I would spend eight years trying to figure that out. Here's what I learned on the journey.

Part 1

The Occult, Wicca, and Witchcraft

There shall not be found among you anyone who makes his son or his daughter pass through the fire, one who uses divination, one who practices witchcraft, or one who interprets omens, or a sorcerer, or one who casts a spell, or a medium, or a spiritist, or one who calls up the dead.

‹ DEUTERONOMY 18:10–11, NAS ›

Chapter 1

THE OCCULT

*M*Y INTEREST IN the occult began when I was young, I remember playing fortune-teller with my friends. We'd be sitting on my bedroom floor in a circle, pretending to read each others' palms. I had an old baby toy. It was round with a clear top and tiny figures in the middle, and you could see through the plastic. My friends and I would take turns gazing into the "crystal ball," looking for what would happen in the future. One day we spent hours trying to read each others' thoughts. I don't know where we learned about psychics or fortune-tellers. My best guess is books from the school library. As a child I thought people who could peek into the invisible world were cool. I suppose it's because I could feel it around me but wasn't sure why or how.

It never occurred to me that trying to do so could be harmful.

Over the years I've watched as our culture has become saturated with the occult. Bookstores provide how-to books on witchcraft, predicting the future, and meeting your spirit guides. Movies romanticize creatures once understood as evil. Television programs explore a multitude of paranormal and supernatural activities.

Psychics, mediums, and supernatural investigators are listed in the phone book.

What I find interesting is how confused Christians are when it comes to the occult. Some seem blinded to the current interest or how it could affect them. Others want to jump in feet first and

explore it for themselves, as I once did. Many Christians don't
have a clue what the occult is.

I'm going to give you the definition I understand:

> *Occult* means "hidden or secret." When speaking about the
> occult, I'm describing belief systems and practices designed
> to uncover hidden or secret spiritual knowledge. Channeling,
> spirit communication, divination, crystals, astral travel, nec-
> romancy, witchcraft, psychic abilities, angel oracles, and so
> forth, are under the umbrella of the occult.

Vacation Bible school was where I first learned we are born into
a sinful world. The Bible tells us in Romans 3:23, "All have sinned
and fall short of the glory of God." No exceptions. My experience
suggests to me that humans are prone toward specific temptations. There may be a peculiar weakness unique to them or their
family that the enemy can exploit. Examples include excessive
drinking, gambling, anger, sexual immorality, jealousy, bitterness, worry, rebellion, stubbornness, envy, gossip, or (in my case)
witchcraft.

In the past few years I've spent a lot of time reading the Bible
and discovering what it has to say about the occult. As it turns
out, there's quite a bit. There are modern words not found in the
Bible. The word *occult* is one of them. There are, however, words
describing proper names or activities that we associate with the
occult.

These words include:

× *Amulets/charms* (Isaiah 3:17–20): Objects/jewelry
that can be worn or carried that have been imbued
with or are believed to hold magickal properties to
bring luck, love, wealth, healing, protection, cursing,
blessing, and so forth.

✕ *Charmer* (Deuteronomy 18:10; Psalm 58:5; Isaiah 3:3; 19:3): One who creates charms or amulets, uses words or sweet sounds (snake charmer), dealing in spells, charms, amulets, and talismans.

✕ *Divination* (1 Samuel 15:23; 2 Kings 17:17; Jeremiah 14:14; Ezekiel 13:6–7; 21:21–22): Using objects or patterns in nature to determine the future.

✕ *Enchanter* (Deuteronomy 18:14; 2 Kings 21:6; Jeremiah 27:9; Micah 5:12): One who uses enchantments, sorcery.

✕ *Familiar spirits* (Leviticus 20:27; 1 Samuel 28:8; Jeremiah 23:32; Acts 16:16): A spirit that provides information to a medium, necromancer, false prophet.

✕ *Magicians* (Daniel 1:20): One who interprets omens and secret things.

✕ *Medium/necromancer* (Leviticus 20:6, 27; 1 Samuel 28:7; 1 Chronicles 10:13): One who conjures and/or communicates with the dead or acts as a mediator through which the dead can allegedly interact with the living.

✕ *Soothsayer* (Joshua 13:22; Isaiah 2:6; Micah 5:12): One who uses various methods to foretell future events; includes receiving supernatural information as a psychic, false prophet, and so forth.

✕ *Sorcerer/sorceress* (Exodus 22:18; Deuteronomy 18:10; Malachi 3:5; Revelation 21:8; 22:15): One who practices divination, conjuring, sorcery, enchantments.

✕ *Sorcery* (Galatians 5:20; Revelation 9:21; 18:23): The
  dispensing of medication, poison; the practice of
  spells, incantations, charms, etc.

✕ *Spells* (2 Kings 9:22; Isaiah 47:9; Micah 5:12; Nahum
  3:4): Sorcery or magickal arts.

One thing stands out to me when I read these scriptures. These
activities (or the people choosing to do them) are condemned. God
clearly states we are not to have anything to do with these types
of activities ourselves or to seek out people who do them for any
reason. I believe we can reasonably deduce that actions, or the
people identified with them, that are similar or of the same spirit
as these (while not specifically addressed in Scripture) should be
considered forbidden.

Modern terms include :

✕ *Witch/witchcraft*: One who believes natural or occult
  forces can be harnessed through spells, charms,
  incantations, and amulets; the practice of magickal
  arts.

✕ *Wicca/Wiccan:* One who practices goddess/pagan
  ritual worship, which may include the use of spells,
  divination, and magickal arts.

✕ *Psychic*: One with a familiar spirit that aids them
  in forecasting the future or revealing hidden
  knowledge.

✕ *Channeler*: One who consults, conjures, or acts as a
  mediator with the dead or foreign spirits.

✕ *Spirit guide*: A familiar spirit that provides information to a medium, necromancer, channeler, psychic.

Here is the big question I asked while looking back on eight years of exploring the occult. Why does God forbid consulting the dead, forcing our will on a situation, or seeking advice from spirits? Simple. It leads us away from Him. We look to ourselves or other spirits for answers only God can address.

What was the attraction to the occult for me?

I was raised in a Christian bubble. Exploring the occult was a chance to break the mold I was used to being in. My own experiences, coupled with exposure to occult ideas, gave me context upon which to build curiosity.

There are many Christians today who are experiencing a similar desire for hidden or secret knowledge on a greater scale. The American religious climate is in upheaval with many young adults leaving the Christian faith. These days it's easier to say, "I'm spiritual but not religious," than to endure public animosity toward the individual or church. Perhaps even worse are those who call themselves Christian while abandoning foundational beliefs about Jesus Christ and replacing them with a more socially palatable solution.

Throughout my life I felt a deep longing to seek out secrets in the world hidden beyond my five senses. No one should tread there lightly. I learned the hard way that a Christian isn't excluded from deception.

My story proves the point.

ꞈ ꞈ DIGGING DEEPER ꞈ ꞈ

Now we see but a poor reflection as in a mirror; then we
shall see face to face. Now I know in part; then I shall know
fully, even as I am fully known.

—1 CORINTHIANS 13:12

1. Why do you believe people are interested in secrets?

2. How do you see popular culture influencing
   Christians today?

3. Do you think it's reasonable for God to forbid occult
   practices? Why or why not?

4. Do you have any experiences (childhood or adult)
   with the occult?

Chapter 2

WHAT IS WITCHCRAFT?

HAT IS WITCHCRAFT?

This is an excellent question, one that people ask me quite often, and it turns out to be the most difficult to answer.

Why? Well, the best answer is because every person who practices the Craft has their own definition. Ask ten witches, Wiccans, or pagans to define witchcraft, and you'll get ten different answers. Sure, there are common beliefs, but there's much diversity. To keep this simple, I am only going to use the standpoint I took on witchcraft when I practiced it.

> Witchcraft is: "Connecting with deity/universe through nature; embracing magick as a way of life."

People think of spells and rituals as being witchcraft, an idea gleaned from popular entertainment and accepted by many who practice it. While there is some truth to the sentiment, it doesn't touch the root of witchcraft. Witchcraft is more than the sum of its practices. Incantations, spells, occult tools, and rituals are a part of witchcraft, but they do not define it. If you want to understand witchcraft, you must go deeper.

Witchcraft is spiritual.

For me witchcraft became the lens through which I viewed the world and the vehicle to express my spiritual leanings.

The transition didn't happen overnight. I waffled between the Craft and the church for years, banging my head against what I called survivor's guilt. This is not surprising. Many people involved in Wicca or witchcraft come from a church background. I found many sojourners who understood my resolve to leave God and Christianity behind.

I attended a Pagan Pride festival a number of years ago. The event was held in a local park. The organizers had all the proper permits so they could offer food, seller's booths for handmade wares, entertainment, and workshops. The entrance fee was a nonperishable item to be donated to a local food bank. The evening was capped with an open ritual circle. The weather was perfect, the festival well attended. The only dark spot on the day was a group of Christians who arrived with a bullhorn and signs, shouting condemnation to passersby. I had to ask two young men to escort me to my car because I'd been surrounded in the parking lot by these "witnesses of the faith." Sadly, this is the kind of display many expect from the church when it comes to witches or Wiccans. Believe me, it hasn't endeared them to hearing the gospel. It's almost a given—if you talk about Christianity to someone practicing the Craft, you'll get a very sullen reaction. Why? They've been wounded.

In my case there was more going on beneath the surface.

I never wanted to admit I felt convicted; the whole idea made me angry. Yielding to temptation felt liberating after years of denial.

I dove into magickal and occultic practices, but concerns niggled at me all the same. What if everything I learned in church was right? How would my children be affected by my spiritual decisions? In those moments I would be gripped with fear, making the hasty decision to be a good Christian again. I'd get rid of all my occult stuff and pretend the religious mask was the real thing. Needless to say, it never took long to go back to my witchy ways because the decision was shallow at best.

I got pretty good at ignoring those nudges from the Holy Spirit, believing "once a witch, always a witch." The sentiment became a sort of mantra for me.

It didn't stop God from pushing the issue, though.

People will ask me, "Why the Craft?", citing witchcraft as a supernatural power trip. Some of it was feeling valued as a woman, on equal footing with my counterparts. There were no restrictions on how I could develop as a spiritual leader. I honestly believed I had control over my destiny. If circumstances (money, health, relationships) didn't work out in the mundane (ordinary) world, I could direct spiritual energy through spell casting to accomplish my goals. If I had an upcoming decision, I could divine (future-cast) potential outcomes for guidance. As a witch I felt rooted to the earth and universe. Years later I recognize the experience for what it was (Isaiah 14:13–14). So yeah—power trip. It was tantalizing to believe the key to everything was found within myself—at least until the true weight of spiritual culpability came crashing down.

Following my decision to return to Christ, I decided to take a closer look at what it meant to be a witch. While reading the Bible, I discovered one interesting exchange, which sums up witchcraft, its practices, and associated beliefs and puts everything I'd ever done as a witch into sharp perspective.

Samuel, the prophet and final judge of Israel, is speaking to the king. Saul was a man who had committed to honoring God in everything. Throughout his reign Saul became increasingly arrogant, resulting in disobedience to God's commands. He got the idea things would be fine so long as he repented later with a sacrifice. However, Samuel had some news for Saul:

But Samuel replied,

"What is more pleasing to the LORD:
    your burnt offerings and sacrifices
    or your obedience to his voice?
Listen! Obedience is better than sacrifice,
    and submission is better than offering the fat of rams.
Rebellion is as sinful as witchcraft,

and stubbornness as bad as worshipping idols.
So because you have rejected the command of the LORD,
    he has rejected you as king."

                —1 SAMUEL 15:22–23, NLT

The truth of those words unmake me every time.

    Rebellion: "Refusing to accept God's authority in my life."
It's the very root of witchcraft.

Let's just say I've stopped pointing fingers at King Saul.

The Bible declares emphatically that God is the only true, living God. As a witch I flouted God's natural authority over my life, first by bowing down to idols and then myself. Divination, sorcery, charms, talismans, spell casting, spirit communication, and the like are practices of witchcraft. God is not empowering those activities, but something certainly is—and it's not benevolent "universal energy."

I got the up close and personal on that regard.

We are in a spiritual battle, and the allure of witchcraft is one small part of it. Satan didn't create witchcraft or any other traditions people have conceived of over the generations. Instead, the enemy exploits man's curiosity for the unknown and desire for spiritual connection. Through witchcraft Satan provides an alternative to God, offering a myriad of elemental spirits and supernatural guides to tempt us into sin. Human beings continue to pursue false promises and reasonable-sounding teachings in spite of God's revealed purpose and plan through Jesus Christ. Thankfully I finally remembered the most important thing before it was too late.

As a Christian I must be utterly dependent on God's grace and obedient to His will.

For me anything else is witchcraft.

↗ ↗ DIGGING DEEPER ↘ ↘

Yet they rebelled
    and grieved his Holy Spirit.
So he turned and became their enemy
    and he himself fought against them.

—ISAIAH 63:10

1. In Isaiah 63:10 it says that the rebelliousness of the people grieved God's Holy Spirit. Why?

2. Do you believe rebellion is the root of witchcraft?

3. Why or why not?

4. How do you define *witchcraft*?

5. Do you think Christians can practice or participate in witchcraft without realizing it?

Chapter 3

MEETING THE GODDESS

*M*Y INTRODUCTION TO Wicca began while reading a library book called *Ariadne's Thread: A Workbook of Goddess Magick* by Shekinah Mountainwater. I was alone, depressed, and searching for answers. The book was a revelation into a world I'd never known and introduced me to a deity I'd never considered.

My first experience with the goddess occurred while raising a cone of power (a vortex of energy).

My children were napping, so I felt free to experiment with a suggested exercise in the first chapter of the book. I sat on the floor, my legs crossed. I spent some time with my eyes closed, breathing. As directed, I moved my upper body in a clockwise circular motion, cleansing myself with white light. I began chanting a sacred sound while visualizing energy swirling up and around me until it closed over the top of my head. The feeling was intoxicating. And then I read the invocation to the goddess.

The response was immediate. She knew me. I was being welcomed into a loving mother's arms.

Enthralled, I wanted to learn more, but my husband was adamantly against it. He understood the ramifications of what I'd been doing. I returned the book to the library. I worked harder at being a Christian. My degree from college is in music performance. I did some professional work, singing background vocals on the debut album of a Christian rock band. I stood up front every Sunday in church with a worship team. Four years would pass before that experience with the goddess surfaced in my mind once more.

My life began falling apart in October 1999. My husband and I had been in financial trouble for a while.

I stayed at home with our children, homeschooling, and there was never enough money. My husband and I were both struggling under the weight of depression and anger issues. I did everything possible to seek God's favor. I prayed, read Scripture, and volunteered at church. No answers or relief was forthcoming. It seemed as though the Father God I'd known from childhood had abandoned me. I was convinced by other Christians that I didn't have enough faith. When my husband declared he was giving up his Christian beliefs, I decided it was time to look for Mother Goddess. I wanted to explore my womanhood from a different perspective than the church provided. I wanted magick and to understand the occult. I was desperate, searching for spiritual refreshment in a religion gone dry. Wicca gave me what I wanted.

What is Wicca? Who are the Wiccans? Why is this mystical religion appealing to so many people?

Wicca is a modern earth-based religion founded on ancient European fertility goddess worship. Wiccans are people trying to connect with the divine who have found a familiarity through reimagined pagan rituals and the lore of ancient deities. They are people drawn by magick because it feels like home.

I remember.

The first thing I discovered about Wicca is that it is duotheistic, polytheistic, and pantheistic. That means the main deities are the Triple Goddess and the Horned God (dual facets of a universal force), represented by various gods and goddesses. There are some monotheistic groups that follow the Great Goddess.

Wicca has a variety of traditions, including:

✕ *Gardnerian*—Created by Gerald Gardner, considered to be the father of Wicca (British Traditional). Generally practiced in a coven of thirteen, membership by initiation through high priest or priestess, secret rituals and practices.

✕ *Alexandrian*—Created by Alexander Sanders (British Traditional). Based largely on Gardnerian tradition, although more eclectic with use of Jewish Qabalah and ceremonial magick elements.

✕ *Georgian*—Created by George Patterson (British Traditional) in the United States. Similar to Gardnerian and Alexandrian. Growing in popularity among the American Armed Forces.

✕ *Celtic*—Incorporates Celtic lore, deities, and seasonal festivals.

✕ *Dianic*—Created by Zsuzsanna Budapest. Feminist and goddess centered, combining elements of British Traditional, folk magick, and Italian folk magick known as Stregheria.

✕ *Nordic*—Incorporates Norse lore, deities, and seasonal festivals.

✕ *Faerie*—Incorporating faerie myth and folklore.

✕ *Eclectic*—Pulling from a variety of traditions, focusing on more than one pantheon. Eclectics often practice alone but can include covens, such as the Georgian tradition.

I chose to follow the Eclectic tradition. There were elements I liked from various paths, but I didn't want to be bound to those traditions as a whole. I was a solitary, never working within a coven. I interacted with the witchcraft community through e-mail and Internet groups and attended festivals. My sacred circles were goddess centric as in Dianic tradition. I used folk magick. I bought books and supplies online. I borrowed ritual ideas or spells from Celtic or Faerie traditions, reworking them to suit my purpose. Wicca encourages people to study for a year and a day before dedicating themselves to the goddess. I studied ancient pantheons and myths surrounding goddess personalities. I memorized correspondences between nature and magick through color, crystal, rock, and leaf. I read as much information as I could on the phases of the moon. I observed Esbats (full-moon rituals) and The Wheel of the Year (Wiccan holidays).

There were two goddesses I was drawn to in particular from the beginning: Artemis (Greek goddess of the hunt) and Brighid (Celtic goddess of the high arts). As I learned how to meditate and cast a sacred circle, I called on these goddesses. Artemis and Brighid each had an altar in my home. I used flowers, herbs, candles, and other natural elements corresponding with their personalities to honor and draw their energy.

They began appearing to me in visions or dreams.

The first time I found myself sitting on a bare spot of earth surrounded by a forest. The intensity of the vision in my mind's eye amazed me. Stars twinkled over my head through the tops of the trees. I could feel a cool breeze caress my skin. There was a small campfire. Across from me sat a woman, whom I recognized as Artemis. A stag stood to her right, while a wolf was seated beside her on the left. A long bow rested across her lap. She stared into my eyes for what seemed like hours. Artemis placed her hands beneath her bow and lifted it from her lap. Reaching over the fire pit, she placed the bow on my lap. She nodded. The vision faded. It was the first of many such encounters.

Brighid was the goddess who named me.

I'd been struggling to find a Craft name. In Wicca it is a tradition to find a name for use while doing magick, rituals, or to claim as your identity as a witch. I'd been searching for my name for a while. I'd tried various word combinations inspired by nature—even a few in Gaelic—but nothing seemed right. One night I had a dream. I saw myself surrounded by a ring of fiery red gemstones. As I sat within the circle, I felt safe, protected. The gems were garnets, my power stone. As I gazed at the brilliant red light encircling me, a woman's voice spoke. She said, "Your name is found within the stones." I'd encountered Brighid in meditation, so I recognized her voice. When I woke up, I knew my Craft name.

Red Krystal.

I was able to keep my occult practices secret from everyone. During the day I was a teacher at a Christian preschool, but at home I was worshipping the goddess. My husband had no idea. I confided in him about the daily meditation I'd begun practicing, but I kept my small collection of ritual supplies in a box in the closet. My husband discovered the truth when he came home one day and found me writing in my *Book of Shadows* (a spiritual journal for recording spells, rituals, and relevant information). He didn't respond other than to pull away even further in our relationship.

A vision from Artemis would encourage me to leave my husband.

I was preparing for a full-moon ritual when suddenly I was in the forest chasing a stag. The long bow was in my hand, a quiver of arrows on my back. When the stag came to rest near a tree, Artemis was there. She wanted me to shoot the stag. I obeyed. As the creature fell to the ground, it became my husband. When I returned to myself, heartbroken, I realized my relationship with my husband was dead. I told him I was leaving. My decision was soon justified upon discovering he was in an emotional affair with another woman.

I left believing I'd found empowerment as a woman through Wicca, but there was a problem. The Holy Spirit poked at my idolatry from the start.

As I've mentioned, waffling became the norm because of the guilt I felt. There was a part of me who loved Jesus and wanted to keep the childhood beliefs I'd known all my life. My problem was getting past the legalism that had come to represent Christianity to me.

Three years into goddess worship the situation came to a breaking point.

My children and I were living with my mother. I was separated but not divorced from my husband.

I'd started exploring the darker goddesses such as Kali and Hecate. I wanted to balance light and shadow in my life. I was feeling content for the first time in a long time. Then my daughter came into my bedroom one afternoon asking if I'd take her to church the next day. My children had been going to my mother's church for two years, but my daughter wanted me to take her. I agreed, although I told her it would have to be a different church. Most of those people at my mother's church had known me since childhood.

The next day as I sat in the pew of a small, anonymous church for the first time in three years, I was uncomfortable. Spending so much time immersed in pagan belief, I disagreed with half of what the pastor said. So it was a surprise when I found myself moving forward for prayer at the end of the service. I confessed goddess worship as a woman prayed for me. For a moment I felt peace. I thought I'd found reconciliation with God and the church. When the service was over, I tried to speak to people, but being a stranger, I was unable to break into their conversations. There was not so much as a "Thank you for coming." My feelings of reticence returned.

I didn't belong in the church.

Now I was faced with a dilemma. The church no longer seemed an option, but I didn't want to worship goddesses anymore either. My confession at the altar was genuine. Wicca was not where I belonged. I'd been leaning in the direction of Solitary Eclectic Witch for a while. I wanted magick but without religion. I wanted Father, Son, and Holy Spirit but without the church.

I wanted my own spiritual path.

I cast a circle, calling out to both Brighid and Artemis, breaking ties with them. I would follow Jesus, acknowledging Him as the Son of God. I accepted parts of the Bible I liked while rejecting the rest. I wouldn't go to church, but I'd make peace with God. It was the first time I considered melding witchcraft with Christianity.

My decision did not set well with one goddess.

As I was getting into bed, I became aware of a female presence nearby. I knew who it was. After all, I'd spent three years getting to know her. She was the goddess who sat across from me time after time in my sacred circle, the one I invoked to enhance my spells.

Artemis was present, and she was not pleased.

In my mind's eye I could see the goddess's normally beautiful features distorting into an ugly visage filled with anger. Waves of hatred flowed toward me, and the message rang clear in my thoughts. Love and patience were no longer extending to me. Everything that was familiar about her was gone.

I didn't know this being.

"You belong to me."

I felt terrified.

Even in my self-imposed deception I think I recognized what was masquerading before me as a benevolent goddess. I chose to ignore the truth. I was unwilling to consider that the spirits fueling my experiences were actually deceiving me.

Assuming Artemis wouldn't go away, I pulled my sheet near my chin, rolled over on my side, and reminded her she no longer had a right to come to me. I was going to be a Christian again. I told her to leave, invoking the name of Jesus. I closed my eyes, aware of her fuming rage a few inches from my feet until she was gone.

Some might explain the incident as understandable. They might argue that after all, I'd walked with Artemis. I had worshipped the goddess in all her aspects for three years before deserting her. She wasn't showing her true nature, but justifiable anger.

I disagree.

The Bible teaches me in 1 Corinthians 8:4–6 (NLT): "We all know that an idol is not really a god and that there is only one God. There may be so-called gods both in heaven and on earth, and some people actually worship many gods and many lords. But we know that there is only one God, the Father, who created everything, and we live for him. And there is only one Lord, Jesus Christ, through whom God made everything and through whom we have been given life."

My final encounter with Artemis proved this to me. I'm thankful that despite choosing to bow down before goddesses, God never abandoned me.

The Holy Spirit pursued me.

A few weeks later my husband called for the first time in over a year. He spoke with our children, apologizing for being absent from their lives. He asked to speak to me. He told me God had given him an epiphany. He'd gotten his faith and life straightened out. He wanted our marriage restored.

My response was not kind or repeatable.

My husband wasn't deterred. He prayed. He called every few days. He found reasons to talk to me after chatting with the girls. He told me what God was doing in his life. I told him I was a Christian again (honestly believing I was). In time he convinced me to try a reconciliation. It was the first of a series of separations and reconciliations before God brought complete healing to our relationship. The same would be true of my spiritual condition.

Delivering me from the idolatry of goddess worship was only the first step.

Today our society believes that to be tolerant of another

person's beliefs or religion means you must agree that all choices, beliefs, and religions are equally true or right. The modern definition of *tolerance* leaves no room for absolute truth but grants people individual versions of truth based on perception. I discovered an important reality. The idea that we can create truth flies in the face of Jesus, who said, "I am the way and the truth and the life. No one comes to the Father except through me" (John 14:6).

Wiccans are good people. They have a genuine desire to live in light and love. And they need to know the good news of the gospel. Wiccans need to experience the love of Christ through His followers. Wicca seeks to reconnect the ancient deities with a new expression for the modern world. The truth is, if you read mythology, you learn that the gods and goddesses were capricious and vengeful. People lived in fear (not awe) of them.

My experience with the goddess taught me this lesson.

God is not fickle. He is relentless in His love for us. The goddess can only offer a pale imitation.

✶ ✶ DIGGING DEEPER ✶ ✶

So in everything, do to others what you would have them do to you, for this sums up the Law and the Prophets.
—MATTHEW 7:12

1. The Wiccan Rede says, "An' it harm none, do what ye will." How does this differ from the Golden Rule?

2. What do you know about Wicca?

3. Do you know any Wiccans?

4. Many Wiccans come from a church background. Why do you think they leave Christianity for Wicca?

5. How do we reach out to people who are following a Wiccan path?

Chapter 4

THE CHRISTIAN WITCH

OVER THE PAST few decades the American church has under-gone radical change. Cultural shifts now influence many denominations. Popular voices question what was once recited as creed. This leaves many confused. Where do you go for answers when the loudest people talking don't seem to have a clue?

I chose to go outside the church. The crazy part was believing I could bring what I'd learned back with me.

I became a Christian witch.

What? Did I lose my mind or my Bible? There is no such thing as Christian witchcraft. The idea of combining the Christian faith with occult practice is ludicrous! Who would believe such a thing was even possible?

Someone influenced by a postmodern society. A person hungry for spirituality without rules.

Me.

The Bible simply became a book of wisdom, literature, and history. I rejected it as the inerrant Word of God, embracing spiritual experience as my guide. When I read Scripture, my focus was on the teachings of Jesus, James, or Peter. I disregarded Paul as a misogynist. The Holy Spirit became mother goddess within the Trinity. The image of wisdom (Sophia) from the Book of Proverbs became a separate feminine aspect of God. Worship was private. I'd cast a sacred circle in my bedroom, the backyard, a park.

I avoided the corporate church experience.

As a witch I lived as naturally as possible. My altar was decorated with herbs or flowers of the season and a cross. Esbat (Full Moon) focused upon the Holy Spirit (Mother; Sophia/Wisdom) and drawing her energy. The Autumn/Spring equinox and Winter/Summer solstice became my primary sabbats. Christian symbolism featured prominently in spell work and rituals. I sought direct answers from God through tarot, the pendulum, and scrying (inducing visions) with a crystal or black mirror. Occasionally I used psalms as incantations for spells. All my Christian beliefs were suffused with magickal practice.

The real question isn't whether Christian witchcraft exists, but why. Discovering how the current trend makes it possible should be the main objective. There are many plausible explanations. I believe the initial spark came from a simple declaration:

"I'm spiritual but not religious."

Five simple words. Using those words, individuals start bucking the traditional church system. They discover ways to express their beliefs without reflecting organized Christianity. An example would be someone who chooses to deepen their experience with God inspired by Eastern religious traditions. What's happening in this instance is called syncretism. The concept is very simple. Spiritual syncretism is the blending of otherwise incompatible belief systems into a unified whole.

This is the foundation for Christian witchcraft.

Some may deny its existence, but doing so is not helpful. The magickal movement within the church might be small, but it is real. Here is what I learned from other Christian witches as I progressed the path.

- ✕ Most Christian witches have a deconstructionist view of the Bible.

- ✕ Christian witches will include the Gnostic gospels as part of their sacred texts.

✕ Archangels, angels, and saints can figure heavily in
   rituals and spell work.

✕ Most Christian witches practice some form of
   divination.

✕ Many Christian witches continue as regular
   attenders in their local congregations.

✕ Most Christian witches hide in plain sight.

Maybe I was a little desperate when I first thought about combining Christianity and witchcraft. I'd spent the previous three
years making a concerted effort to retrain my thinking to adopt
a polytheistic worldview. I took great pleasure in everything I did
within witchcraft and the occult.

I liked being a witch.

My pastor would call that indulging the soulful flesh. I was cool
with it at the time. The problem was the constant war with my
pesky spirit! One thing became painfully clear. I couldn't keep
vacillating between two disparate belief systems.

It would be another two years before I found my answer.

I was attending a Spirit-filled church and working as a teacher
for another Christian preschool at the time. One day, on a whim,
I searched the Internet for *Christian witch*. My jaw dropped when
I saw the results. There were thousands of websites devoted to
my quest. Here was evidence of other people forging their own
magickal path while holding on to Jesus. I wasn't alone!

The recurring motto was: "There are more of us than you think."

One site in particular seemed to offer everything I wanted—a
community message board that included seekers (those wanting
to learn how to meld Christianity and witchcraft), apprentices
(those in process of learning), and adepts (people competent to
teach others). The webmistress offered a thirteen-moon Internet
apprenticeship for students she believed possessed an innate

knowledge of witchcraft. She followed a traditional witchcraft path, trained by aunts and a grandmother in Brujeria (Spanish) and Stregheria (Italian) folk magick.

She accepted six students per year.

I spent days reading this woman's articles. Her writing was confident. I wanted to learn from this woman, although I wasn't sure if she'd accept me. I wasn't what some would call a hereditary witch. I didn't know if I possessed what she called witch blood, but I wanted to find out. Everything she wrote affirmed what I believed about myself. I downloaded a long application form, completed answers to the best of my ability, and submitted it.

The waiting was interminable. I began to worry the webmistress hadn't received my e-mail or was refusing me as a student. The day I discovered her reply in my in-box my heart was pounding. She accepted me as a student for an eight-moon study. She would decide afterward whether to receive me as an apprentice.

I was elated!

The study went something like this. My mentor would e-mail me a lesson each month. I had time from New Moon until Full Moon to complete the questions and exercises. I'd send everything back for evaluation, observation, guidance, and suggestions for deeper study. I would receive her response and new lesson before the next New Moon.

I loved studying Christian witchery with my mentor. The lessons, questions, and activities were interesting, thought provoking, and challenging. She taught me to examine my Christian beliefs and to recover forgotten soul knowledge of witchcraft.

She taught me to view the natural world as an ally. For instance, I spent one entire moon studying a single plant. I took pictures of the plant, found it in a field guide, and studied its growth pattern. I learned if it had any safe-use medicinal purposes for brewing teas or tinctures. I spent time with its energy, discovering what assistance could be offered in magick. In a similar way I learned how to sense the course of the moon by studying each phase, sensing the change in energy as the moon waxed and waned.

My mentor didn't believe in the need for such things as wands, goblets, cauldrons, or other trappings found in Wicca. She had no objection if a witch enjoyed using stuff for rituals or spell craft as a focal point, but she emphasized magick from the mind's eye. I was already good at visualization. Her lessons taught me to hold an image in my mind with more clarity and greater lengths of time.

She offered group classes and discussion topics on her message board. I joined groups discussing tarot, herbs for spell craft, ritual suggestions, and the like.

My mentor showed me traditional "Christian witchery," but her goal was to open my eyes, not give me a how-to. She gave me exercises to discover my shadow self and understand the darker aspects of my nature. Through it all I shared my deepest thoughts about the past and what I hoped for my future with a woman I never met.

Because she was teaching me witchcraft from a Christian viewpoint, she challenged me with an intense study of words in Hebrew and Greek. Working with her, I gained a better knowledge of church history. She reviewed traditional teaching about witchcraft and magick in a way that appeared elegant and reasonable. She expounded on the differences between witchcraft and Wicca. More than once she dismissed my work as a medium and ghost hunter. She believed Scripture was wrongly interpreted in regard to magickal practice but was correct in its denunciation of mediums. However, she insisted I make up my own mind by examination of Scripture and through prayer.

It was our only point of contention.

Time passed. I was accepted into my mentor's thirteen-moon study. When she began mentioning the use of psychotropic herbs or plants such as peyote, I decided I needed a break. I've never been comfortable with the notion of being out of control of my body. I was a social drinker, but I never used drugs. The very idea of what she was asking made me nervous. I wanted to be sure I was ready before I delved any deeper. Explaining this, I took several months to process everything I'd learned. Once certain of my direction I e-mailed my mentor, informing her of my intention to continue under her tutelage. She was happy, promising to send a *Moon* in the next day or so.

Anticipating the upcoming lesson, I was surprised when nothing materialized in my in-box. I waited a week before e-mailing my mentor again. I received an automated response explaining she was ill and would be in contact soon.

I never heard from her again.

My mentor's websites and blogs were removed from the Internet. She no longer posted on forums or message boards. She vanished. I was saddened to lose her counsel but otherwise content. I focused my energy on pursuing the Christian witch path, increasing my ability as a medium, and being a ghost hunter.

The sudden removal of a mentor from my life is what I like to call a God thing. Four months later I was delivered from the snare of the occult.

In today's spiritual climate syncretism is gaining traction. I believe the church's perceived image problem has a lot to do with it. Christianity has fallen short of expectation. I disagree with certain dogmas about the traditional role of women. I am disappointed by the politicization of Christian teaching and leadership.

The greater church body has no idea what the Scriptures say. The Bible is the most widely sold, owned, and translated book. Ever. Yet most Americans who claim to be Christian have never bothered to read it. They make assumptions about their beliefs based on what they hear from the pulpit or popular media—a situation that leads people into doing what feels right while ignoring the truth.

For as long as I can remember, I have perceived the spiritual world that surrounds us. Even as a child I experienced the presence of God in worship. I saw His angelic servants. I witnessed the activity of demons. I experienced gifts of the Holy Spirit as God allowed. I remember as a teenager talking to my pastor about this.

He reminded me to always base my faith on Scripture and not spiritual experiences alone.

I wish I'd heeded his warning.

Syncretism allowed me to believe I could be a witch and right with God despite all biblical evidence to the contrary. The truth is I could have chosen any other belief system. The result would have been the same in the end.

Self-deception.

⤝⤝Digging Deeper⤞⤞

Show me the right path, O Lord;
   point out the road for me to follow.
Lead me by your truth and teach me,
   for you are the God who saves me.
   All day long I put my hope in you.
Remember, O Lord, your compassion and unfailing love,
   which you have shown from long ages past.
Do not remember the rebellious sins of my youth.
   Remember me in the light of your unfailing love,
   for you are merciful, O Lord.

—Psalm 25:4–7, NLT

1. Have American Christians deviated from Christian teaching? How or when did this transition of belief happen?

2. Can you be a Christian if you accept beliefs from other religions as your own?

3. How much influence does culture have on the church?

4. Can you think of examples of syncretism in your own life?

5. What do we need to do as Christians to make sure we are staying on the right path?

Chapter 5

CREATOR OR CREATION?

I HAVE ALWAYS HELD a deep appreciation for God's creation. You could even call me a nature lover, but not in a camping, hiking, roughing-it-in-the-woods kind of way. My husband thinks it's because I was raised a country girl. As a child I spent most of my days outside. In summer I'd pick black raspberries and gather honeysuckle. In fall I'd tromp through the bright-colored forest to a bare spot of ground, armed with an empty tin can, bits of colored wax, string, and a box of matches, to make sand castles. Snow-packed winter found me skating on frozen ponds or tobogganing down hills. Spring was spent splashing through mud puddles and listening for peepers to begin a croaking serenade. As an adult I grow herbs, admire thunderstorms, and gaze at stars.

> The heavens declare the glory of God; the skies proclaim the work of his hands.
> —PSALM 19:1

> How many are your works, O LORD! In wisdom you made them all; the earth is full of your creatures. There is the sea, vast and spacious, teeming with creatures beyond number—living things both large and small.
> —PSALM 104:24–25

> For since the creation of the world God's invisible qualities—his eternal power and divine nature—have been clearly seen, being understood from what has been made, so that people are without excuse.
> —ROMANS 1:20

In pagan and witchcraft tradition nature is not viewed as the creative work of a transcendent God. Nature is the divine mother that sustains us. Every leaf and seed pod, insect or animal has its own spark. The dirt and rocks upon which humans tread pulsate with universal energy. All life on earth is connected. A pagan, Wiccan, or witch will worship in nature where the goddess, god, and elemental spirits are entreated to join the sacred circle. A witch can ally herself with nature, attune to its rhythms. In doing so, the witch is further empowered in spell craft.

As a witch I wanted to revere and protect the earth mother. Believing nature was part of the divine made sense to me. Circumstances dictated that my sacred circles took place inside my bedroom, but whenever possible I'd be outside. I'd call upon the guardians of north, south, east, and west to protect and work with me. I'd invoke the elements of earth, air, fire, and water. Being outdoors made the connection seem that much more powerful. Anytime a public pagan event was held in a local park, I made sure to participate in the open circle.

My favorite meditation was sitting in my backyard and focusing on the trees. I sat cross-legged on the lawn, my hands resting easily on my knees. I slowed down my breathing and visualized my personal energy stretching from my toes, past the blades of grass, digging deep into the earth. I would then shift my gaze to a tree, observing the bark and imagining the roughness beneath my fingertips, watching the leaves rustle in the breeze. Soon I would "see" an aura of energy spread out little by little. Closing my eyes, I continued to see the ethereal tree in my mind's eye while I listened to the wind as it shifted around me, the tree, creating routes through the atmosphere. I eventually visualized and traveled along them astrally. I was the tree, the wind, part of the energy of the universe. Through these visualization exercises I learned the fundamental elements of spell work and how to live on the witch path.

As a Christian I view nature differently. I know I'm meant to be a steward. I'm to care for God's beautiful creation with a sober mind. I can do this by conserving energy, using biodegradable products, buying local farm produce, recycling, changing my diet to be vegetarian or vegan. I can adopt a pet from a shelter. I can make sure my footprint is as small as possible. As a Christian I need to care about our planet. I can respect nature. I can appreciate a glowing sunset. The main thing is to keep proper perspective. God alone is worthy of praise. Nature itself proclaims His glory if we take the time to notice.

> You will go out in joy
>   and be led forth in peace;
> the mountains and hills
>   will burst into song before you,
> and all the trees of the field
>   will clap their hands.
>
> —ISAIAH 55:12

> He existed before anything else, and he holds all creation together.
>
> —COLOSSIANS 1:17, NLT

How foolish I once was to think a stone was anything more. How could I deny the One who proclaims Himself by leaving His fingerprint on my very DNA? When I think about it now, I am astonished by my own willfulness. I may not have carved an idol, but I fashioned gods of my own design all the same. I desired a connection to spiritual forces that have nothing to do with God.

> A fool has no delight in understanding, but in expressing his own heart.
>
> —PROVERBS 18:2, NKJV

People attach spirit and intelligence to trees and rocks while ignoring the living God—the One who has done everything for our benefit and held nothing back, securing our redemption because of His great love.

◢ ◢ DIGGING DEEPER ◥ ◥

For since the creation of the world His invisible attributes are clearly seen, being understood by the things that are made, even His eternal power and Godhead, so that they are without excuse, because, although they knew God, they did not glorify Him as God, nor were thankful, but became futile in their thoughts, and their foolish hearts were darkened. Professing to be wise, they became fools.
—ROMANS 1:20–22, NKJV

1. How do you think Christians should view nature?

2. What kind of role does nature play in your life?

3. What do you believe motivates a person to worship creation instead of the Creator?

4. How can we balance respect for nature with reverence for God?

5. What does being a steward of God's creation mean to you?

Chapter 6

MAGICK: NOT PRAYER WITH PROPS

*M*AGICK IS PRAYER with props." I had been a recommitted Christian for a couple of years the first time I read those words. I'd started writing a blog called *Kristine ReMixed*. I hadn't been telling people my story up to that point. When I felt the tug to start writing about my experiences as a witch, my husband suggested the blog. I was creating a post on the differences between prayer and magick when I ran across the statement on an open forum. How could anyone believe two such distinct concepts were identical? As a witch I understood the difference between magick and prayer.

So, what is magick?

First I can tell you what magick *is not*. Magick is not sleight-of-hand trickery, illusion, or what's represented in popular books, television, or movies. Magick is spiritual...an activity performed in the mundane world that intersects with the spirit realm...intentional design weaved into being through intangible art.

The difference between magick and prayer is witnessed in spell casting.

Spell casting directs intention to bend energy for a desired outcome. Power is added to a spell when the caster joins with nature or deity. Items such as essential oils, gemstones, natural objects, and candles can be used based on corresponding symbolism or energy. Days of the week, phases of the moon, time, and season can play a role in the execution of a spell.

As a witch I used candles carved with runes for many of my spells. I didn't need to use props; no experienced spell caster does. I simply enjoyed the ritual. I chose the color based on the desired outcome and then anointed the candle to narrow my focus. When it was time, I'd cast a sacred circle, ground and center myself, and meditate. I invoked spirits and deities to strengthen the energy surrounding my intent. Concentrating on the candle flame, I would then shape the spell in my mind before sending it into the universe with spoken words. I was confident of the results.

Magick is as real as the deceptive beings that empower it. My spells were successful because they validated the ruse these spirits used to convince me I was powerful. The snare tightened with every spell I cast. As a witch I could manifest my own spiritual desires as reality. I could believe in God or not.

Prayer is different.

Prayer is worship, an expression of faith, an opportunity for confession and surrendering concerns. Prayer doesn't and shouldn't demand its own way. Through prayer a person yields to God.

In Luke 11:1–4 Jesus is asked by His disciples how to pray:

> One day Jesus was praying in a certain place. When he finished, one of his disciples said to him, "Lord, teach us to pray, just as John taught his disciples." He said to them, "When you pray, say:
>
> "'Father,
> hallowed be your name,
> your kingdom come.
> Give us each day our daily bread.
> Forgive us our sins,
>   for we also forgive everyone who sins against us.
> And lead us not into temptation.'"

The Lord's Prayer is a model of how we are meant to pray. Jesus doesn't want me babbling useless words into the ether.

He wants a conversation. I'm designed to seek God. His will, not mine. I trust Him to provide for my needs. I mess up; He's there to help. I am wronged; He shows me how to forgive. He gives me strength when I am tempted. When the enemy knocks me down, I get back up because Jesus extends an outstretched hand. What I experienced as a witch (and medium) was a parody of the relationship I have with God. Magick assisted the self-indulgent way of living I had adopted. When I did pray, the imposters tried to deafen my ears to the true God.

His voice would not be silenced.

I love to talk to God. What's more important, I know He listens and responds—maybe not the way I expect, but He always responds. Prayer is now a lifestyle for me. I pray any time, any where, eyes open or shut, speaking or silent, laughing or crying. I can raise my voice in concert with other believers. I can pray while walking the dog, picking berries, driving the car, or grocery shopping. My prayers are often expressed through song and the written word. When words fail, prayer becomes movement or is found at the stroke of an artist's brush.

Not long ago my husband and I struggled with finances. Worry was beating us both into the proverbial ground. I was scheduled to attend a local worship and art night, but I didn't want to go. Friends were sponsoring the event, so I felt obligated to make an appearance, but my attitude was awful. I didn't want to risk complaining when I was supposed to be celebrating. As I got into the car, I started praying.

"Lord, I can't think straight because I'm so stressed. Help!"

I decided to play a CD recording of the Bible during the short drive to the event. The CDs were sitting next to me on the seat. Grabbing the one on top, I shoved it into the player on the dashboard. I had no idea which one I'd picked. Soon an actor's voice filled the air loud and clear:

That is why I tell you not to worry about everyday life—whether you have enough food and drink, or enough clothes to wear. Isn't life more than food, and your body more than clothing? Look at the birds. They don't plant or harvest or store food in barns, for your heavenly Father feeds them. And aren't you far more valuable to him than they are? Can all your worries add a single moment to your life?

And why worry about your clothing? Look at the lilies of the field and how they grow. They don't work or make their clothing, yet Solomon in all his glory was not dressed as beautifully as they are. And if God cares so wonderfully for wildflowers that are here today and thrown into the fire tomorrow, he will certainly care for you. Why do you have so little faith?

So don't worry about these things, saying, "What will we eat? What will we drink? What will we wear?" These things dominate the thoughts of unbelievers, but your heavenly Father already knows all your needs. Seek the Kingdom of God above all else, and live righteously, and he will give you everything you need

So don't worry about tomorrow, for tomorrow will bring its own worries. Today's trouble is enough for today.

—MATTHEW 6:25–34, NLT

My eyes welled with tears. Peace and comfort flooded me as I listened. I was able to worship that night with the people in attendance. Near the end of the evening I shared how God used His Word to answer my plea. A person in a similar situation approached me. My story encouraged her. The evening was a success, and I had a renewed perspective on my situation.

God doesn't always intervene in such a direct manner when I pray. Most of the time I figure out His response through daily devotional reading or taking a step of faith when the way seems open. I might hear a confirmation through a pastor's teaching or a trusted friend. Sometimes I know God's answer because my spirit is uneasy. Even when I have to wait years, God never leaves me hanging.

Prayer is communication.

Magick is self-serving.

A prayer might ask for God's intervention, but His will alone determines the outcome. A spell instructs the universe what the caster expects to be done. Many traditions in Christian denominations involve a candle or incense. Advent candles burn while scriptures are recited and songs sung in remembrance of Jesus's birth. We break bread and drink wine (or grape juice) while reflecting on His sacrifice. As a child I had the opportunity to light the candles on the altar for my church's worship service. These examples could be construed as prayer with props. None bridge the gulf between spell craft and prayer.

Traditions can hold significant value without being magick.

The important thing I remember when I go to pray is to be genuine. When my prayers start sounding like a "honey do" list, I take a step back. The point of prayer is fellowship with God. Prayer affords me the opportunity to grow as my faith is stretched and tested.

Prayer is knowing God.

⚞ DIGGING DEEPER ⚟

This is the confidence we have in approaching God: that if
we ask anything according to his will, he hears us. And if we
know that he hears us—whatever we ask—we know that we
have what we asked of him.

—1 JOHN 5:14–15

1. Has this chapter altered your view on either prayer
   or spell casting?

2. Is it wrong to light a candle as a symbol of prayer?

3. How do you define prayer?

4. Is it possible to tell God what to do?

5. Do you feel like God is approachable?

Chapter 7

EASTERN MEDITATION: GATEWAY TO THE OCCULT

I WAS SITTING ON the floor of my darkened bedroom. My kids were watching television while my husband played on the computer in the living room. The only light came from a candle in front of me. I'd been studying Wicca for several months. The books recommended visualization exercises to sharpen focus and manipulate energy. Meditation was suggested to learn about self, deity, and the universe.

Eastern meditation has grown in popularity through yoga and is recommended as a therapeutic treatment by doctors. The idea is to relax breath and body so the mind can move beyond common awareness. Meditation doesn't empty the mind so much as dismiss conscious thoughts so a practitioner can be in the moment.

There are a variety of methods for meditation. Some people gaze at a focal point. Others use repetitive sounds such as *Om,* a sacred word, or a chant until they reach an altered state of consciousness. Some religious meditations include ecstatic movement or singing.

I participated in a ritual where ecstatic dance was employed. The drumming music started slow. A fair-sized group of women, we moved into position. When the ritual began I was standing, but I ended on my knees. It was easy to drift with the rhythm. Over time the intensity of the beat increased, as did our movement. Some hit the ground with fists; others whirled like dervishes. I swayed, contorting my body to reflect the sounds I was hearing. Emotions roiled within me, building to fever pitch before a final exhausted release. The ritual was designed to be a cathartic exorcism of inner demons. I remember lying on my mat later with the sensation I was in a void.

Reflecting on the experience, I'm reminded of Jesus's teaching:

> When an evil spirit leaves a person, it goes into the desert, searching for rest. But when it finds none, it says, "I will return to the person I came from." So it returns and finds that its former home is all swept and in order. Then the spirit finds seven other spirits more evil than itself, and they all enter the person and live there. And so that person is worse off than before.
> —LUKE 11:24–26, NLT

When a yoga studio provided free space for kirtan, I attended for over a year. *Kirtan* is devotional singing of mantras dedicated to Hindu deities. The activity induces a meditative state. I loved it! Once a month we met in a room decorated with several small shrines. We'd lay our mats on the wood floor, settling ourselves in quiet anticipation. We started with personal meditation until a recording began to play. The main singer would introduce the mantra as we sang with the response chorus. The mantras were in Sanskrit. Sometimes we had words and translations printed but not always. The repetitive nature of the exercise broke the language barrier. Most of the songs began with a slow cadence, increasing in volume, speed, and instrumentation through the middle before winding down for another. Kirtan was blissful. I felt open and relaxed at the end of each meditation session.

Now I understand how vulnerable I was.

I enjoyed meditation from the start. Practicing twice a day helped me learn how to focus. Once I learned what worked for me, I could sit for an hour just existing. Visualization and meditation became an essential part of my life as a witch and medium. Everything I came to believe was validated through meditation.

There were times when I had out-of-body experiences. One evening I felt myself drift up and out of my body, hovering over the candle. I could see white energy surrounding me as I looked down. Needless to say, I was shocked back to normal awareness. Over time I learned to enjoy it as a peaceful sensation, although I never sought it on purpose.

Christian meditation is very different.

It is an active reflection upon scripture—a way to imprint God's Word in my memory and spirit. The mind isn't divorced from the body but engaged in learning about God's nature. By focusing on key passages or verses, pondering what the words mean in context, I can apply those principles to my life.

The Bible is the living Word of God (*rhema*). The distinct voice of the Holy Spirit is present throughout. He will use Scripture to illuminate new meaning into verses even if I've read them a thousand times. In this way the Bible is my lynch pin in determining what is or isn't from God.

Second Timothy 3:16–17 tells me: "All Scripture is God-breathed and is useful for teaching, rebuking, correcting and training in righteousness, so that the man of God may be thoroughly equipped for every good work."

Joshua 1:8–9 reminds me: "Do not let this Book of the Law depart from your mouth; meditate on it day and night, so that you may be careful to do everything written in it. Then you will be prosperous and successful. Have I not commanded you? Be strong and courageous. Do not be terrified; do not be discouraged, for the LORD your God will be with you wherever you go."

I find it vital to meditate on Scripture daily.

What I practiced for eight years as a witch and medium was designed to bring me to serenity. Christian meditation is meant for spiritual health and growth. Without the foundation of Scripture it's all too easy to fall prey to any distorted truth.

> And many will turn away from me and betray and hate each
> other. And many false prophets will appear and will deceive
> many people. Sin will be rampant everywhere, and the love
> of many will grow cold. But the one who endures to the end
> will be saved. And the Good News about the Kingdom will
> be preached throughout the whole world, so that all nations
> will hear it; and then the end will come.
>
> —MATTHEW 24:10 14, NLT

I see people in the church falling into the same traps I did. I
hear them expound on Christian spirituality using the repetition
of a sacred word such as *Jesus* or *Lord*. Many Christians are practicing contemplative prayer, centering prayer, or soaking prayer,
which are heavy with mysticism.[1] I've read the explanations for
including these under the mantle of Christian meditation. Sacred
words and contemplative prayer achieve an emotional response—
but to whose god?

Because these forms of meditation are identical to what I
learned as a witch and medium, I won't practice them.

As a Christian witch I used Psalm 46:10, "Be still, and know
that I am God," to justify Eastern meditation. In reality the verse
has nothing to do with inner reflection but rather with how the
nations will acknowledge God as sovereign. I used the verse out
of context to advocate believing if something felt good, it must be
from God.

That sentiment is not always true.

There is a desire to be quiet before the Lord in prayer or worship. I understand. There is nothing wrong with approaching
God, actively seeking His response. We don't need to superim-
pose Christian meaning to esoteric spiritual methods to achieve
that goal.

Hindsight allows me to see many ways the enemy can infiltrate
a Christian's life. Confusion over Eastern meditation is one of
them. I know it's easy to get excited when spiritual things happen.

There is nothing so sweet as witnessing God's miraculous hand at work. But I know how the enemy can twist that expectation, causing experiential encounters to overshadow wisdom.

Christian meditation on Scripture allows me to recognize the truth from a lie when employed with discernment.[2] This is how God interacts with us and helps us learn His voice. My relationship with God is strengthened day by day because of it.

⌁ ⌁ DIGGING DEEPER ⌁ ⌁

Let the words of my mouth and the meditation of my heart be acceptable in your sight, O LORD, my rock and my redeemer.
—PSALM 19:14, ESV

1. What does meditation mean to you?

2. Do you meditate? Why or why not?

3. Do you think people accept experience over Scripture? Why or why not?

Chapter 8

DIVINATION AND
FAMILIAR SPIRITS

I WAS ALWAYS CURIOUS about the future.

You may recall that as a child my greatest ambition was to be a Gypsy fortune-teller. My favorite Halloween costume for years included my mother's dress swirled with bright colors, a knit shawl, a paisley scarf wrapped around my head, and gold hoops dangling from my ears. Fortune-tellers were cool. What I didn't understand was that reading palms or gazing into a crystal ball was a practice known as divination.

Divination is future-casting using specific tools designed to intersect with supernatural sources to reveal information. As a witch and medium I employed various forms of divination when seeking direction in my life.

Divination is an ancient practice and includes a variety of disciplines. Methods include:

× *Astrology*: A system based on the alignment of the stars and planets in relation to birth dates. Zodiac symbols and horoscopes are the most recognizable product of astrology.

× *Numerology*: Computing a series of numbers that have special significance based on a number assigned to a person's name or other sources.

X *Geomancy*: Interpreting the patterns of thrown dirt or the ground.

X *Palmistry*: Interpreting the lines and creases in the palm or shape of the fingers.

X *Runes*: An ancient Northern European alphabet inscribed on small stones deciphered by the position in which they land when rolled and tossed.

X *Scrying*: Visions induced by gazing into a bowl of water, a black mirror, or crystal.

X *Tarot*: A deck of seventy-eight cards placed in formations. Predictions are interpreted by the cards' location in the spread and how the cards relate.

X *Tea leaves*: Determining the shapes of leaves left in the bottom of a teacup.

X *Pendulum*: A form of dowsing using a crystal or weighted object suspended from a chain or string. The answers to questions are determined by the direction of the swing. Pendulums can be used for diagnosis, finding objects in the earth, locating mineral deposits, indicating hot spots in paranormal investigation, and communicating with spirits.

X Other forms of divination include dream interpretation, reading omens, and others.[1]

Divination is as common today as it was in the ancient world.

I read horoscopes in magazines and identified myself as a Pisces years before I became a witch. Future-casting practices have even passed to us through history as harvest festival games. Did you ever try to pare an apple in one long strip? Tradition says if you drop the peel into water, it will form the letter of the one you will marry. This is an example of divination.

As a witch I spent hours learning divination methods. I explored palmistry. Tarot became a form of meditation for me. I learned how to cast runes and scry with a mirror or crystal sphere. I practiced dream interpretation on friends. Astrology or numerology were too much like math, so I asked others to interpret charts for me.

My affinity was for the pendulum.

Pendulum requires a steady hand so the swing of the suspended object is not affected by finger or wrist. The pendulum answered when I spoke aloud or thought my question. I marveled at the force of the swing and how it came to an abrupt stop as soon as I commanded it. I became a collector of handcrafted pendulums. Each one was unique and beautiful. They were created from a variety of stones designed to draw specific "energy" dependent on my need. I used a crystal-point necklace as a visual aid for my team when I worked as a medium on paranormal investigations. Major life decisions were made based on what I divined with my pendulum.

I was in the middle of another separation from my husband. My children and I had moved with the help of a church we had attended while my husband and I were still together. I wanted a job at a child-care center I had worked for the previous year.

The church provided us a furnished place to live and a well-stocked pantry the day we moved in. Nobody at the church or school knew about my witchcraft. Months before I'd told the pastor it was a thing of the past, a confession I'd meant at the time. Despite the church's good intentions, the neighborhood we lived in was rough. My husband was moving to another state and urged me to go live with my mother again. My children were miserable.

By this time I had convinced myself I could be both a Christian and a witch. I needed to make a quick decision so my children could begin a new school year. Out came the pendulum. When

I asked if I should return to my mother's home, the answering swing was yes. When I asked if the church would find me another home, the answer was no. When I asked if I should stay at the church, the answer was no. When I asked if I should stay at the school, the answer was no.

I chose to leave.

People from the church and school tried to help. They encouraged me to stay, but I refused to listen. My decision was clear according to the pendulum. Years later, I discovered the church was preparing another apartment for me and my children, one in a good neighborhood and school system that would be rent-free for six months. The pastor who came to talk with me the night before I left didn't tell me. I don't blame him. Throughout the meeting I was hostile toward him and his wife, angry at what I viewed as interference. Now when I think about that meeting, I regret not allowing God to work in my life through those generous people.

My first introduction to the pendulum came through a popular television show about a family, set during the Depression. The oldest sister was awaiting the birth of her first child. Her mother, sisters, and ladies from their church were giving her a baby shower. One of the ladies offered to "divine" the sex of the baby by stringing the expectant mother's wedding ring on some thread and swinging it over her belly. The same character also read tea leaves for all the partygoers.

Does it surprise you a television program would depict a good Christian woman practicing divination?

Why not? The episode portrayed reality. My grandfather used divining rods to locate water on his farm. I remember the day he taught me how to water witch. We walked around the yard until we found a thin y-shaped stick. He showed me how to hold the extending branches while waiting for the long end to pull me in the right direction. I didn't find water that day, but it didn't matter. I felt a kind of energy. I thought the exercise was fun.

I loved my grandfather. He was a good man who went to church every Sunday. In his mind water witching was a trick learned as a child, not dabbling in the occult. I've thought about family history while examining my lifelong attraction to the supernatural. I believe familiar spirits were passed to me through dowsing and use of a Ouija board before I was born.

Two years after I became a witch, I attended a witchcraft convention near my home. There were workshops to attend. My favorite Wiccan author was the guest speaker. She offered classes on how to live a magickal life every day. The event took place on Imbolc—a fertility festival held on February 1 or 2 honoring the goddess Brighid and celebrating the approach of spring. You probably know it as Groundhog Day. There were vendors set up to sell their wares. A number of psychics and mediums were available for readings. As I walked through the event, I passed a table where a woman standing behind it blurted out, "You have a parade of spirits following you. I've never seen anything like it!"

I smiled. She only confirmed what I already knew. I communicated regularly with those spirits, using a pendulum before I developed as a medium. Divination was an avenue that opened psychic abilities for me. It gave me a sense of control. The reality is that demonic (familiar) spirits influenced every step I took.

Speaking from firsthand experience, divination is dangerous. Its practices are based on pagan traditions and open a world God never intended us to investigate.

> When you enter the land the LORD your God is giving you, be very careful not to imitate the detestable customs of the nations living there. For example, never sacrifice your son or daughter as a burnt offering. And do not let your people practice fortune-telling, or use sorcery, or interpret omens, or engage in witchcraft, or cast spells, or function

as mediums or psychics, or call forth the spirits of the dead. Anyone who does these things is detestable to the LORD. It is because the other nations have done these detestable things that the LORD your God will drive them out ahead of you. But you must be blameless before the LORD your God. The nations you are about to displace consult sorcerers and fortune-tellers, but the LORD your God forbids you to do such things.

—DEUTERONOMY 18:9–14, NLT

People still seem to be looking to find God in ways He's never condoned. Scripture shows me how God interacted with His people (Israel) in the past. He directed their choices as needed by lot (Acts 1:24–26). God instructed Moses and Aaron in the creation of the Urim and Thurim worn by the high priest (Exodus 28:30). God spoke to the prophets (Ezekiel 7:1) and revealed Himself to them in visions (Numbers 12:6). God showed Joseph the meaning of other people's dreams.

"Interpreting dreams is God's business," Joseph replied. "Go ahead and tell me your dreams."

—GENESIS 40:8, NLT

Daniel asked for prayer when confronted with interpreting King Nebuchadnezzar's dream because he knew it was God who would show him the meaning:

Then Daniel returned to his house and explained the matter to his friends Hananiah, Mishael and Azariah. He urged them to plead for mercy from the God of heaven concerning this mystery, so that he and his friends might not be executed with the rest of the wise men of Babylon. During the night the mystery was revealed to Daniel in a vision. Then Daniel praised the God of heaven and said: "Praise be to the name of God for ever and ever; wisdom and power are his."

—DANIEL 2:17–20

God forbids the use of divination. He rejects psychics, mediums, and false prophets who have given themselves over to foreign spirits. The good news for me was deliverance through Jesus Christ. He set me free from the familiar spirits who followed me—spirits who would eventually harass me every day. God put a stop to all of it when I returned to Him.

He can do the same for you.

✐ ✐ DIGGING DEEPER ✐ ✐

Then they all prayed, "O Lord, you know every heart. Show us which of these men you have chosen as an apostle to replace Judas in this ministry, for he has deserted us and gone where he belongs." Then they cast lots, and Matthias was selected to become an apostle with the other eleven.

—ACTS 1:24–26, NLT

1. What do you know about divination? Have you ever practiced it wittingly or unwittingly?

2. Why do you think people are interested in knowing the future?

3. What do you know about familiar spirits?

4. If God opposed divination, why did He communicate through dreams, visions, and prophesies?

5. Why did God speak to His people through lots?

Chapter 9

PRODIGALS CAN ALWAYS COME HOME

EVERYONE HAS A story.

It doesn't matter who you are or what you do. We all go through difficult times in our lives. Jobs are won and lost. Families struggle to relate. Husbands and wives lose their way. How we respond to these experiences will often determine if we're going to grow or get stuck.

There were times I believed it was impossible to return to God.

Drowning in shame, I would gather all the items associated with my witchcraft—a cast-iron cauldron used for burning incense, a large conch shell, lapis lazuli, moss agate, and amethyst stones handpicked for what they represented in my spell casting, my handcrafted wand or *Book of Shadows*, and a small crystal sphere used for scrying. I'd throw them out or give them to witches I knew. I wanted my heart to be in it. I wanted to please God by being good enough. But the moon would move through her phases. I'd find myself staring at the Bright Lady, longing to draw her down.

"Once a witch, always a witch."

And the accoutrements of the Craft would find their way into my possession once more.

People write to me with their own stories of guilt and struggle. "How can God possibly forgive me?"

Jesus showed us the way.

There was a man who had two sons. The younger one said to his father, "Father, give me my share of the estate." So he divided his property between them. Not long after that, the younger son got together all he had, set off for a distant country and there squandered his wealth in wild living. After he had spent everything, there was a severe famine in that whole country, and he began to be in need. So he went and hired himself out to a citizen of that country, who sent him to his fields to feed pigs. He longed to fill his stomach with the pods that the pigs were eating, but no one gave him anything.

When he came to his senses, he said, "How many of my father's hired men have food to spare, and here I am starving to death! I will set out and go back to my father and say to him: Father, I have sinned against heaven and against you. I am no longer worthy to be called your son; make me like one of your hired men." So he got up and went to his father.

But while he was still a long way off, his father saw him and was filled with compassion for him; he ran to his son, threw his arms around him and kissed him. The son said to him, "Father, I have sinned against heaven and against you. I am no longer worthy to be called your son."

But the father said to his servants, "Quick! Bring the best robe and put it on him. Put a ring on his finger and sandals on his feet. Bring the fattened calf and kill it. Let's have a feast and celebrate. For this son of mine was dead and is alive again; he was lost and is found." So they began to celebrate.

Meanwhile, the older son was in the field. When he came near the house, he heard music and dancing. So he called one of the servants and asked him what was going on. "Your brother has come," he replied, "and your father has killed the fattened calf because he has him back safe and sound." The older brother became angry and refused to go in. So his father went out and pleaded with him. But he answered his father, "Look! All these years I've been slaving for you and never disobeyed your orders. Yet you never gave me even a young goat so I could celebrate with my friends. But when this son of yours who has squandered your property with prostitutes comes home, you kill the fattened calf for him!"

"My son," the father said, "you are always with me, and everything I have is yours. But we had to celebrate and be glad, because this brother of yours was dead and is alive again; he was lost and is found."

—LUKE 15:11–32

Prodigals can always come home.

Freedom found me the day I realized I was not bound to witchcraft. When I agreed in my spirit that God was right and that I had missed the mark but the penalty was covered, the Father was waiting. He was scanning the horizon for the day I realized I could come home, and He ran to welcome me into His loving arms.

I promise. God is waiting for you too!

You don't have to do anything to get ready for the journey. Just come home! Don't look back or think about what others might say. Don't worry about the stuff you've left behind. You can haul that to the garbage heap later. Have no fear of recrimination. God wants nothing more than to draw you into His forgiveness and grace. He's waiting to reveal your true identity as an adopted son or daughter.

If we confess our sins, he is faithful and just and will forgive us our sins and purify us from all unrighteousness.

—1 JOHN 1:9

People tell me they left the church for paganism or witchcraft because they didn't feel at home in the church.

My faith is about relationship with God through Jesus Christ. He is my home. God is whom we respond to when the Holy Spirit calls, not a religion. I have found that by fixing my gaze on the Savior, all the church stuff will sort itself out.

So what about you?

Are you ready to come home?

⸙ ⸙ DIGGING DEEPER ⸙ ⸙

For God loved the world so much that he gave his one and only Son, so that everyone who believes in him will not perish but have eternal life. God sent his Son into the world not to judge the world, but to save the world through him.

—JOHN 3:16–17, NLT

1. Do you ever feel like there is something you've done that God can't forgive?

2. Are you a Christian? If yes, what does being a Christian mean to you?

3. Have you ever gone out of your way to avoid God?

4. Why don't people feel at home in the church?

5. Are you a prodigal son or daughter? Would you like to come home?

A SPECIAL PRAYER FOR PRODIGALS

Hi, Father.

I know it's been awhile since You've seen or heard from me. I'm sorry. I got it into my head to go out into the world and experience the pleasures found there. I wanted to taste, see, know, and touch the hidden things that I realize now are dangerous for me. You always told me I could get hurt messing with stuff I didn't understand, but I didn't want to believe You.

I believe You now. You were right...about everything. Please forgive my willful arrogance and attempts to do life on my own. Please forgive me for missing the mark.

I need You. I trust You. I want to be in Your house again. I am Yours. Can I come home?

Thank You! Your love overwhelms me. Your grace amazes me. Your mercy is my freedom. I love You so much. Thank You for loving me. You are my Lord.

In Jesus's name, amen.

PART 2

GHOSTS, MEDIUMS, AND THE PARANORMAL

When men tell you to consult mediums and spiritists, who whisper and mutter, should not a people inquire of their God? Why consult the dead on behalf of the living?

‹ ISAIAH 8:19 ›

Chapter 10

Pursuing the Paranormal

*N*OT THAT LONG ago interest in the paranormal was considered left of center. People absorbed by the study of ghosts, monsters, and aliens were a little odd. Sure there were movies about the birth of Satan's son or stories featuring tormented spirits, but it was never taken seriously in polite society.

These days one in three Americans believe in ghosts.[1] Young adults are more likely to accept that ESP and haunted houses are real than their older counterparts. People in general are inclined to believe in the existence of aliens over God.[2]

I remember watching television specials about Big Foot or the Loch Ness monster as a child. Alien abduction and UFO reports became popular when I was in high school. Past-life stories began to attract attention around that time too. As Eastern mysticism has taken root in our culture, concepts such as Karma or the Buddhist Wheel of Life have become appealing.

People are going to hypnotherapists for past-life regression to understand current emotional issues. As a witch I embraced the Westernized concept of reincarnation. The opportunity to recycle to this earth as a different person was a thrilling idea. I didn't want to give up the tastes, sounds, and colors of life. I think I was a little afraid of dying—without Christ. Reincarnation gave me an odd (albeit false) sense of hope that I wouldn't simply wink out of existence.

Ten years ago a psychic told me I had been a "healing woman" in a former life. She said I was hanged as a witch, and that explained my lifelong aversion to wearing anything tight around my neck (a fact I hadn't shared with her). Her assertions made sense to me. My belief in past lives was strengthened several years later when I had a memory of being four years old and looking at my hand and thinking, "I am very small now." I accepted the thought as a moment of recognition—moving from a past-life sense of self to the next. I discounted what the Bible says about life and death as irrelevant compared to that memory.[3]

There was a popular science fiction TV program of the 1990s that fanned the flames of belief in me as well. It underscored the parallels between UFOs, alien abduction, psychic abilities, ghosts, and other aspects of the occult as paranormal.

I think it's important to understand why people are interested in the paranormal rather than dismiss them out of hand. Where did their beliefs originate? If people have had unusual experiences, what have they done to understand what happened to them? How have their ideas about God or the paranormal been changed as a result of their experiences or exposure to occult ideas? Have they been discouraged or encouraged in their exploration?

Once upon a time I wanted to believe there was life on other planets. I remember having a conversation in college with another student who insisted the Book of Ezekiel was a description of an alien encounter.

> As I looked at these beings, I saw four wheels touching the ground beside them, one wheel belonging to each. The wheels sparkled as if made of beryl. All four wheels looked alike and were made the same; each wheel had a second wheel turning crosswise within it. The beings could move in any of the four directions they faced, without turning as they moved. The rims of the four wheels were tall and frightening, and they were covered with eyes all around.
>
> When the living beings moved, the wheels moved with them. When they flew upward, the wheels went up, too. The spirit of the living beings was in the wheels. So wherever

the spirit went, the wheels and the living beings also went. When the beings moved, the wheels moved. When the beings stopped, the wheels stopped. When the beings flew upward, the wheels rose up, for the spirit of the living beings was in the wheels.

—EZEKIEL 1:15–21, NLT

I didn't understand the nature of prophetic language, so he almost had me convinced. Now as I study Scripture I understand that what is being described by the prophet is a vision of God's throne. I've learned that trying to insert a science-fiction model into the meaning of these verses distorts the richness of Ezekiel's prophetic narrative.

In reality, there is little evidence to support the idea of extraterrestrial life. Well, intelligent life, that is. While microbes or evidence of water on Mars is interesting, neither can be defined as a herald of an alien civilization capable of space travel. This doesn't stop people from embracing it as a probability. In the past fifty years many have claimed to be in contact with extraterrestrial beings through channeling. Others believe life on earth was "seeded" through aliens. The suggestion seems to be that humans are a big science experiment. Some people have reported being abducted by these visitors as well.

Here is what bothers me. I've noticed that people who have these experiences (communication or abduction) never seem to question who these "aliens" might be. It seems to be accepted that "intergalactic scientists" or "benevolent beings" from some galaxy far, far away have nothing better to do than buzz our air space and steal people.

I did some reading on UFOs and claims of alien abduction. Several articles suggested common factors among alien abduction reports. The most notable factor is the high percentage of those who have previously been involved with the occult or New Age movement. Even more interesting are those who come from a Christian background who are left questioning their faith. Many of these adopt a nonbiblical view about God based on their experience.

I'm struck by the fear and trauma these abduction events cause individuals. Similar trauma is reported by people experiencing a haunting. Those who have had "alien contact" and "spirit channeling" proclaim they are receiving messages from benevolent beings who want humans to reach the next stage of spiritual evolution. Their "wise counsel" universally denounces the gospel as standing in the way of world unity.

I don't know about you, but that sounds awfully familiar.

> How you are fallen from heaven,
>   O shining star, son of the morning!
> You have been thrown down to the earth,
>   you who destroyed the nations of the world.
> For you said to yourself,
>   "I will ascend to heaven and set my throne above God's
>   stars.
> I will preside on the mountain of the gods
>   far away in the north.
> I will climb to the highest heavens
>   and be like the Most High."
> Instead, you will be brought down to the place of the dead,
>   down to its lowest depths.
> —ISAIAH 14:12–15, NLT

His tail swept away one-third of the stars in the sky, and he threw them to the earth. He stood in front of the woman as she was about to give birth, ready to devour her baby as soon as it was born.

She gave birth to a son who was to rule all nations with an iron rod. And her child was snatched away from the dragon and was caught up to God and to his throne. And the woman fled into the wilderness, where God had prepared a place to care for her for 1,260 days.

> Then there was war in heaven. Michael and his angels
> fought against the dragon and his angels. And the dragon
> lost the battle, and he and his angels were forced out of
> heaven. This great dragon—the ancient serpent called the
> devil, or Satan, the one deceiving the whole world—was
> thrown down to the earth with all his angels.
>   —REVELATION 12:4–9, NLT

I believe there will be increased interest in paranormal pursuits as mysticism becomes accepted. In fact, I see it happening now. As a result there is greater deception in the world and among Christians. People are adopting explanations that dismiss God or put Him on the periphery. There is a greater willingness to believe anything if it sounds good or plausible.

This trend should be troubling to the church. We can't ignore the paranormal. As Christians we also should not develop an unhealthy interest in the supernatural. Our only option is to understand these issues from a biblical perspective. Anything else is playing into the enemy's hands.

What can I say? I've learned from experience.

⟋ ⟋ DIGGING DEEPER ⟍ ⟍

"Let not the wise man boast of his wisdom
    or the strong man boast of his strength
    or the rich man boast of his riches,
but let him who boasts boast about this:
    that he understands and knows me,
that I am the LORD, who exercises kindness,
    justice and righteousness on earth,
    for in these I delight,"
    declares the LORD.
                                        —JEREMIAH 9:23–24

1. What do you believe about aliens? Why?

2. Why do people find the paranormal interesting?

3. Have you ever had a past-life regression? What do
   you believe about reincarnation?

4. Why do some people have paranormal experiences
   and others never do?

5. How should Christians respond to people who say
   they've seen a ghost or alien?

Chapter 11

Spirits: Angels and Demons

As a ghost hunter I went on many investigations. Our team was always ready to check out places rumored to be haunted—cemeteries, historic sites, homes. We would receive a request for a case, and off we'd go.

The question was—and is—what were we hunting?

There is an invisible spirit world that surrounds the physical one in which we live. In this spiritual world beings exist on a level we cannot fully comprehend. The Bible categorizes these beings into two groups: angels and demons.

Angels are the servants of God. I've learned about them from the Bible. Angels are not human beings who have been given elevated spiritual status. They are created spirit beings—ministering spirits. Angels can appear to humans when required. They are powerful and focused on doing God's will. Angels never accept worship for themselves. God sends angels to guide, protect, provide, rescue, encourage, answer prayer, and care for believers.[1]

I was ten when I saw an angel.

The day was sunny and beautiful. I was playing outside, happy, making up songs about how much I loved God. Wandering into the backyard, I was brought up short by the sight of a being made of brilliant light. The spirit looked like a man wearing a golden sash around his waist. I knew he was an angel. He didn't speak, but I got the message. God was saying, "I hear you; I love you." And then the angel was gone. I remember blinking, looking over my shoulder in the opposite direction. The sun blinded me. Accepting the experience for what it was, I went on with my games. I didn't tell anyone about the visitation until years later.

As a child I had the proper perspective about angels. As an adult I lost my way. When I was a Christian witch, angels were invoked for my sacred circle. This opened the way for a spirit guide, calling himself Archangel Michael, into my life. I wasn't alone in this skewed perception of angels. People go to psychics for messages from angels. Angel oracles have been created, which act like tarot cards. Snapping "angel orb" photos has become popular in recent years. Many claim angelic visitation in the form of feathers, gold dust, or gemstones mysteriously appearing during worship. They claim it's proof of God's presence. In my view, seeking these manifestations is a risky proposition. It distracts people from the true purpose of worship.

> Don't let anyone condemn you by insisting on pious self-denial or the worship of angels, saying they have had visions about these things. Their sinful minds have made them proud, and they are not connected to Christ, the head of the body. For he holds the whole body together with its joints and ligaments, and it grows as God nourishes it.
> —COLOSSIANS 2:18–19, NLT

Demons are altogether different. I've learned about them as well. Demons are created spirit beings who used to be angels but followed Lucifer (Satan) into rebellion against God. The Bible identifies them as unclean, fallen, and angels of the devil. They are listed as "powers and principalities" that we wrestle against. Demons recognize Jesus as the Son of God and must obey His commands. They are powerful and want to be worshipped. Demons cannot escape the punishment for their rebellion. They lie, steal, destroy, and draw people away from God.

Demons were the spirits surrounding me as I grew up.

When I was six, my family moved from the city to the country. I was excited the day we moved into the house, until I ran into what would become my bedroom. A spot in front of the closet made me uneasy. As time passed, I sensed a presence there. I was aware of it watching me while I played. For years I dreamed of a dark figure hovering over me. Waking up, I'd sense it was still there, waiting for something. I chose to ignore it. The demon manifested itself when I was sixteen.

One night as I got into bed, I felt overwhelmed by fear. I could sense that familiar dark presence standing at the foot of my bed. I assumed ignoring it would cause the spirit to leave as usual. This time was different. There was loud breathing. The mattress dipped as if someone was sitting down behind my back.

I jumped out of bed and raced into my mother's room. I woke her and told her what had happened. She sent me to the guest room and went into my room to pray. A short time later my mother joined me in the guest room for the rest of the night. The next day she called our pastor. He came the following Sunday to pray, commanding the spirit to leave in Jesus's name. He prayed a blessing over the room. The demon never troubled me again.

That incident alone should have taught me not to become involved in the occult.

I asked a question at the beginning of this chapter: What kind of spirits was I hunting? Experience and Scripture have convinced me that haunting spirits are demons masquerading as "beings of light" in order to deceive the living (2 Corinthians 11:14–15). I've discovered they will appear in whatever manner best turns an individual away from God. Demons are deceptive spirits bent on our destruction by any means necessary.

I watched a report on television about ghost hunting a few years ago. A pastor was interviewed. He gave a short but succinct answer about ghost hunting: God says don't mess with it. He expressed the same opinion I have about ghosts. The reporter confronted a medium with the pastor's objections to ghost hunting and spirit communication. She responded by saying Jesus appeared to His followers as a spirit. She saw no difference between the postresurrection appearances of Christ and a haunting.

As I read the account of Jesus's postresurrection appearances to the disciples, I see no comparison to ghost sightings. Jesus had marks where the nails pierced His flesh, which His disciples could touch. He ate food and walked with them. When Jesus appeared among His disciples, He assured them He was alive.

> See My hands and My feet, that it is I Myself; touch Me and see, for a spirit does not have flesh and bones as you see that I have.
> —Luke 24:39, NAS

Jesus was no ghost.

This is the hope I have as a Christian. No medium will need to act as a go-between. I'll need no other to point the way to the other side. I won't be tapping on walls or whispering in recorders for ghost hunters.

There is a famous quote by C. S. Lewis in *The Screwtape Letters* that I believe we as Christians should take to heart. In the text Mr. Lewis is addressing the issue of demons, but I think this bit of wisdom can be aptly applied to the spirit world in general.

> There are two equal and opposite errors into which our race can fall about the devils. One is to disbelieve in their existence. The other is to believe, and to feel an excessive and unhealthy interest in them.[2]

Angels and demons are very real. They are an unseen part of the universe God created. As Christians we should be aware of them but resist overindulging our interest in either.

⟋ ⟋ DIGGING DEEPER ⟍ ⟍

So we are always confident, even though we know that as long as we live in these bodies we are not at home with the Lord. For we live by believing and not by seeing. Yes, we are fully confident, and we would rather be away from these earthly bodies, for then we will be at home with the Lord.
—2 CORINTHIANS 5:6–8, NLT

1. What do you believe about angels? What do you believe about demons?

2. Why do demons pretend to be "angels of light"?

3. Have you ever had an encounter with an angel or demon?

4. How should Christians respond to a haunting?

5. What do you believe about life after death?

Chapter 12

ORIGINS OF A GHOST HUNTER

*L*IKE MOST PEOPLE my views about ghosts and haunted places were traditional while growing up. I believed ghosts were human spirits—not that I talked to many people about the subject or my experiences. I assumed people would think I was weird.

In the past ghosts were not a great conversation starter.

I was eleven years old when I wondered if the dead could haunt the living. I was in the fifth grade, transitioning from young child to preteen, a time when complex ideas about the world and a "bigger picture" were taking shape in my thoughts.

Believe it or not, I had deep spiritual discussions with a couple of kids who sat next to me in school whom I didn't even know until that year. The teacher's seating arrangement placed us together. My desk mates and I discovered we had similar interests, including the supernatural. One afternoon during free time we began discussing ghosts. What does a ghost look like? Was it strange to be a ghost? Did it get boring watching people who were still alive?

I never told anyone about the spirits in my room or the dreams I had, not even my desk mates that year. Books and movies suggested ghosts were dead people. I understood angels from Bible stories. The spirits I knew frightened me. I didn't connect them with the idea of ghosts.

Ghosts seemed safe by comparison.

I flirted with the idea of inviting a ghost to visit me, but I decided against it in the end. Instead, as we passed cemeteries in the car, I'd duck down, and at night I started pulling covers over my head to hide. There were no sound reasons to tempt fate.

As a teenager I learned about EVPs while watching a TV special about ghosts.

An EVP (electronic voice phenomenon) can occur through recording devices used while communicating with the dead. Nobody knows what an EVP is or how it works. The basic idea is that spirit voices can be heard in the background static or white noise of a recording. Research into capturing the voices of the dead began as early as the 1920s during the spiritualist move-ment. As technology developed, paranormal investigators made use of analog recorders. Today most ghost hunters use digital recorders as part of their investigative procedure.

EVPs can be divided into three classes:

× *Class A*: Loud, clear, and easy to understand

× *Class B*: Understandable but lacking clarity or volume

× *Class C*: A voice is present but hard to hear or understand.

EVPs are unnerving. The one I heard on television had a whis-pering voice that sounded forlorn. Chills tingled down my spine, yet I felt sorry for the ghost and wished I could help. My interest was piqued.

As a witch it seemed natural to improve my ability to sense spirits. I wanted to communicate with them. In 2005 ghost hunting was a new form of entertainment. Watching real-life paranormal investigators gave me the courage to believe I could become one. An Internet search located the group I would later join.

People ask me, "Why ghost hunting?"

Ghost hunters seek to prove (or disprove) anecdotal and

legendary accounts of paranormal activity. I wanted to help people understand ghosts and spirits. I wanted to share my own stories. I wanted an explanation for experiences I'd had most of my life.

Becoming a ghost hunter made sense.

I contacted the founder of the group via e-mail and introduced myself as a clairsentient (clear-sensing) person. We spent a month corresponding and swapping stories. One day he invited me to join the group on an investigation. They were going to several cemeteries rumored to be haunted, as well as a spot associated with a local legend.

I met them at dusk in the parking lot of a grocery store. We introduced ourselves, checked equipment, and formed a small caravan to the first location. As I stepped through the gate of the cemetery, my senses burst open. Prickles enveloped the soles of my feet, traveling up my body to the crown of my head. My stomach began to gnaw and rumble. The darkness seemed to grow deeper around me. The rest of the team was moving toward the first few granite headstones dotting the ground, but I stopped.

My feet felt rooted.

I'd been to cemeteries in the past. As a Girl Scout I went to an old graveyard with my troop to rub charcoal over paper for etchings off the stones. I'd seen my grandparents and several friends laid to rest. On such occasions I focused on the ceremony, family, or friends. There was something in the background, but I chose to ignore it. Now I was seeking it out. I exposed all of my senses to the unseen world. The clarity was stunning. I could detect spirits everywhere. Some gave the impression they'd been hanging around for a while. Others were drawn by our visit. The energy of their individual presence made the tiny hairs on my arms rise. I could "see" them in my mind's eye.

Shaking myself, I hurried to follow the team leader.

"I'm feeling a little weird. I got nauseated as soon as I passed the gate."

He nodded, adjusting the shoulder straps of the two equipment bags he was carrying.

"Yeah. A lot of people report that happening here."

The group began dispersing throughout the area in pairs. Flashlight beams bobbed along the ground into the blackness. Markers set with flower wreaths, flags, and tokens of remembrance were briefly illuminated as someone would stop to read the name.

As we walked farther in, the team leader recounted the story of the woman in white who supposedly haunted the cemetery. The story dated to the 1800s when the woman and her lover were caught in a tryst by her husband. Enraged, the man stabbed his wife. The two men died while grappling over the knife. Hunters and young couples claim to have been witness to a spectral reenactment of the deaths ever since. Some report glimpsing the woman walking down the road passing the cemetery.

The overwhelming sensations I experienced upon entering the location dissipated. I trailed the leader, indicating where to focus his video recorder or camera when I felt a strong surge of spirit energy near me. This became our pattern throughout the rest of the night. When we approached the grave marker of the woman suspected of being the lady in white, I was filled with a righteous indignation not my own. The old stone was worn and broken, the inscription hard to read. I looked at the team leader.

"This woman isn't your ghost. She died a natural death. She wants to make sure you know that too."

The team leader looked at me.

"You sure?"

I nodded my head, and he shrugged.

"Well, OK then."

My assertion proved correct two years later when deeper research concluded the woman died of typhoid fever.

We stayed at the cemetery for several hours before returning to our cars and moving to the next location. The process repeated at the other cemeteries we visited. Much of the evidence (orbs or mist columns) captured that night came from areas I indicated. When the team leader told me the news a few days later, it confirmed in my mind I was on the right path.

Our last stop that night was a place called Hell's Bridge. The legend focused on an old iron bridge where it was rumored a man had committed atrocities and murdered children. The man was caught and condemned to death when local townspeople followed him to the bridge one evening. Before his death the man blamed his actions on demonic possession.

The bridge itself was located at the end of a long trail in a remote wooded area. We walked single file along the path. As we neared the place, a feeling of dread began to well up within me. The team leader had only given me vague details on the story, so I was surprised by a sudden desire to turn and run in the other direction. As we broke through the treeline, I understood. There was an ancient presence attached to the place. Reluctantly I followed the group as they began to make their way across the bridge. As I stepped off the rickety metal extension onto the grassy bank, I became dizzy.

Evil oozed from the ground.

The air seemed thick. My skin itched with a repugnant loathing. I retreated to the other side of the bridge within minutes. I kind of freaked out. My body was trembling. I started babbling what I was "seeing" to anyone who would listen. Apparently, I gave the name and description of a little girl at some point. I don't remember doing that. The team leader shared the details a year later when another medium confirmed the information during a visit to Hell's Bridge, which I missed.

The creepy bit happened when I got home after that first investigation.

I had a really sweet dog named Dakota, an Australian Shepherd/

American Husky my girls and I rescued from an animal shelter. Whenever I came home, she would greet me with joyful enthusiasm. Dakota would run up to me, stick her head between my knees, and stay there until I vigorously petted her shaggy sides. When I came through the door after being at Hell's Bridge, she stopped in her tracks before reaching me. Her ears bent down against her fluffy head, tail tucked between her legs. Dakota backed away, hiding as if she was terrified of me. I didn't see her until the next morning. When she finally approached, she was tentative. She never reacted that way again when I came home from an investigation. You'd think such an unusual occurrence would have given me pause about my activities. Animals are traditionally considered sensitive to crazy stuff. I was so exhilarated from my ghost-hunting experience I dismissed the dog's behavior as a fluke.

As I worked with the group, my abilities intensified. We were doing a home investigation. While outside I received a message from a spirit waiting in the house. She was inviting me in. There were other mediums in the group that night. We tag-teamed during vigils (séances), including one in the upstairs bedroom where I sensed the female spirit. Her name popped into my mind. I spoke it aloud in unison with one of the other mediums. We opened our eyes, smiling at each other. Those in-sync moments were always fun. I also sensed the presence of the client's grandfather in the home. I could "see" him in the den. He was watching TV with the family, a favorite activity while alive. Later the client showed me the closet in that room where the urn holding her grandfather's ashes was kept.

Let me share how a typical ghost hunt was conducted by my group.

A client would contact our group for an investigation. The case manager would ask the client a series of questions to determine the type of paranormal activity being alleged. The case manager then would investigate the property, search for a history, and provide information for the team before the investigation.

The day of the investigation team members would take a baseline reading of the location using EMF (electromagnetic field) meters, note electrical boxes, outlets, and exposed wiring. They would take a video recording and digital photographs of the location.

The mediums would then arrive at the location to perform individual readings. We were the only ones who were told nothing in advance. We didn't receive any information or talk to the client or each other about the location until our readings were complete. One member of the team would follow the medium with a video recorder during the reading. The medium carried a small hand-held digital recorder. Once all the preliminaries were complete, the team would meet and determine the hot spots based on the confirmed readings of the mediums. Then the equipment was set up.

We spent a minimum of an hour at each hot spot. For the EVP work we would ask questions aloud while recording, leaving time for answers. We'd notate fluctuations in temperature and EMF. We videotaped and recorded each vigil. The members of the team would make note of any personal experiences such as phantom drafts, touches, shadow people, voices, taps, footsteps, and so forth. We would also make note if nothing happened.

As a medium I would get information as a flash of "knowing." There were rare occasions I might hear a word, laugh, or footstep. I perceived spirits in my mind's eye, but sometimes I saw an apparition. During investigations where we experienced intense activity, I would use a pendulum so the others could verify answers I was receiving from spirits based on the direction of the swing. Depending on the nature of the haunting and reaction of the client, we'd offer a house blessing or prayer before ending the night. We'd spend days going over the data, recording our conclusions, and creating a report for the client.

Television makes it seem as if ghost hunters make contact with spirits or capture evidence every time they go out. Reality is quite different. Our investigations could be pretty boring. The mediums would sense no spirit activity. Nothing registered on the EMF. There was no evidence on the recorders, digital cameras, or video. We'd debunk every claim to the relief of some clients and consternation of others. We had plenty of investigations where nothing happened, but that rare 10 percent kept us going.

When I rededicated my life to Christ, I started looking in the Bible for answers to the strange experiences I had undergone. Now when people ask, I share what I have learned about discernment, the true identity of ghosts, and the cause of a haunting. Many Christians who have formed their own ghost-hunting groups don't want to hear what I have to say.

Should Christians become ghost hunters? As a former medium and ghost hunter, my answer is NO.

> When men tell you to consult mediums and spiritists, who whisper and mutter, should not a people inquire of their God? Why consult the dead on behalf of the living?
> —ISAIAH 8:19

Christian ghost hunters respond, "We don't consult or use mediums on our investigations. We don't conjure spirits!" Are you sure? The *Merriam-Webster Dictionary* defines *conjure* as: "to summon by or as if by invocation or incantation."[1]

Here's my take on that definition and how it applies to ghost hunting:

× Asking a ghost questions in the hope of receiving an answer via EVP is invoking a response.

× Soliciting a manifestation for the purpose of capturing an image or response qualifies as a summons.

✗ Using modern technology does not change the fact
that spirits are being sought out for communication
and revelation.

"Ghost hunting," I've been told, "is not conjuring up spirits but
dealing with what is still here."

When I read the Bible, I'm led to a different conclusion.

In Luke 16:19–31 Jesus tells the story of a rich man and a beggar
named Lazarus. Lazarus dies, and angels carry him to Abraham
(a representation of being in heaven). The rich man goes to a place
of separation and judgment. He's not allowed to leave the place
he's in. No one from heaven is allowed to go to him. The rich man
asks if Lazarus could be sent to his brothers to warn them. The
answer is no. The dead do not have the freedom to go wherever
they want. The Bible tells us there is a "great chasm," which neither side is allowed to cross. Furthermore, returning from either
place is characterized as "rising from the dead," not making an
appearance as a ghost.

So you tell me. If Scripture makes it plain that when humans
die, they either enter God's presence or go to a separate place, how
can any human spirit be responsible for the effects of a haunting?
Are we going to suggest God is incapable of getting people where
they are meant to be upon their deaths?

A few months after I gave up ghost hunting, someone asked me
if I quit because it had taken an emotional toll on my life. No. The
truth is, I loved ghost hunting. I wanted to be a medium. What I
didn't realize was the subtle influence the enemy exerted through
my ghost hunting and medium activities. I thought I was following God's will for my life.

He made sure I discovered the truth.

⟋ ⟋Digging Deeper ⟍ ⟍

Have nothing to do with the fruitless deeds of darkness, but
rather expose them.
—Ephesians 5:11

1. Why are some Christians drawn to activities such as
   ghost hunting?

2. Are Christians who get involved in paranormal
   investigations compromising their faith or witness?

3. How can a Christian help someone who claims to
   have paranormal activity in their home?

4. What should you say to a Christian who believes
   ghost hunting is a form of ministry?

5. What do you believe about life after death?

Chapter 13

DANGEROUS GAMES

WHEN I WAS young, the best thing in a girl's life was a slumber party; sleeping bags, junk food, gossip, and staying up to all hours made for an exhausting but fun adventure. The highlight of the evening was a spooky game.

We'd kneel in a circle on the carpeted floor of a darkened room, a bunch of skinny girls in flowered cotton PJs. One of us would volunteer to lie in the center of the circle on her back, her arms rigid against her sides. Flashlights positioned around the outside of the circle illuminated our faces in an eerie glow.

The air was charged with the electricity of our collective anticipation.

We placed hands palm up, tightened into fists with the first two fingers extended, beneath the volunteer, just touching the fabric of her nightgown. Eyes screwed shut, we'd begin the chant, muttering over and over, "Light as a feather, stiff as a board. Light as a feather, stiff as a board."

Do you have any similar memories?

Séance or psychic games were popular in the 1970s. I imagine finding ways to scare the pants off your friends hasn't changed much over the past forty years. It's practically a rite of passage into adulthood. Most children go along with these group activities, even if they're scared spit less.

Be honest. Who hasn't been alone in a dark room chanting "Bloody Mary" or "Mary Worth" while staring into the mirror with the intent of raising something behind your reflection in the glass? My sister and her teenage friends used to dare each other to do it. After all, it's nothing more than a simple mind game or parlor trick.

Isn't it?

Skeptics boast that nothing comes of playing with a spirit board or other occult games. Any testimony of uncommon experiences during these games is explained away as induced hypnosis, group hallucination, or muscle spasms.

People believe occult games are harmless fun.

Did you know Ouija boards are considered suitable for children ages eight through twelve? They come in many fashionable colors. You can get one in pink or glow-in-the-dark black. Voodoo dolls are available in the toy section of some online retailers. Tarot, oracle, and pendulum kits are sold as games as well. Did you ever play with a Magic 8 Ball? My friends and I had all kinds of fun asking it questions to learn the future.

Have you ever looked into the origins of these toys and games?

The Magic 8 Ball was inspired by a spirit-writing device used by the inventor's clairvoyant mother.[1] The urban legend game Bloody Mary (aka Mary Worth) closely resembles a fertility ritual. A young woman would look into a reflective surface to see the man she'd marry while risking a peek at the face of death.[2]

The levitation game I described at the beginning of this chapter is attributed to children in seventeenth-century London during the plague. The person in the center of the circle is simulating a dead body.[3]

Here is my point.

Playing with a Ouija board or voodoo doll, participating in a séance, summoning a spirit—even as a party game—is dangerous. Most of the time the only consequence is a sleepless night, but spiritual doors in children's lives may still be opened. Occult games leave a person susceptible to deceptive spirits who may beguile or harass them when they least suspect it—sometimes years after the fact.

Poke the spirit realm long enough, and you will probably get a reaction.

When I think about my life, I see so many places where my interest in the supernatural was tweaked through seemingly harmless fun. We can't ignore the ungodly influences in our world. We dismiss occult games because we don't look deeper than what's accepted by our society.

Many find my warning about these children's games ridiculous. I ask you to consider what is meant to be the greater influence— the church or the culture in which we live? Teaching children to forgo a typical slumber party tradition such as "Light as a feather, stiff as a board" may seem insignificant, but if your child is shown wisdom and follows it, he or she may be spared from a darker path.

⟋ ⟋ Digging Deeper ⟍ ⟍

Now the Holy Spirit tells us clearly that in the last times
some will turn away from the true faith; they will follow
deceptive spirits and teachings that come from demons.

—1 Timothy 4:1, NLT

1. Have you ever played an occult game? What kind of
   game was it?

2. Have you had an unusual experience as the result of
   participating in an occult game?

3. What do you believe is the attraction of occult party
   games?

4. Should children be allowed to play with a Ouija
   board? Why or why not?

5. Do you believe the Magic 8 Ball should be included
   as an occult game? Why or why not?

Chapter 14

GHOST STORIES

ONFESSION TIME; I love ghost stories.

Do you remember those slumber parties from childhood I spoke about? Well, spooky games weren't the only thing we did to scare each other. We told ghost stories—"The Monkey's Paw," "The Hook," "The Signal Man"—the standard classics, which one girl was sure to tell with great dramatic flair. Holding a flashlight under her chin, the storyteller's voice would grow softer and softer until the crucial moment when she yelled into the faces of her avid listeners.

Belief in ghosts, an afterlife, haunting, or vengeful spirits can be traced back to ancient cultures such as the Greeks, Romans, Chinese, and Egyptians. The Bible makes it quite clear to me that the ancient Hebrews were aware of the spirit world.

One of the earliest ghost stories was recorded by a Roman senator known as Pliny the Younger (A.D. 61–115). His tale has all the classic earmarks of what we consider a proper ghost story. There was a restless spirit, clanking chains, and the ultimate resolution of laying a body to its proper rest.

Ghosts are part of humanity's shared cultural experience. They appear in fictional literature in such works as William Shakespeare's *Hamlet*, Charles Dickens's *A Christmas Carol*, and Washington Irving's *The Legend of Sleepy Hollow*. In the modern era the horror novel is widely popular. Television and movies are well-known sources for frightening tales. It's important to note that the common factor in all ghost stories, past and present, is a personal encounter.

I've had many paranormal experiences, which could be told as a traditional ghost story.

One day I was home alone in my bathroom preparing for a shower. My daughters and I were living with my mother at the time. She had taken the girls on a special outing—lunch and a little shopping—allowing me some much-needed time to myself.

As I pulled a towel from the cupboard, I heard what sounded like heavy footsteps stomping up the stairs, moving past the bathroom door and into my adjoining bedroom.

I was a little startled.

Thinking my mother had forgotten something, I peeked out the window into the driveway, but my car was the only one there. Puzzled, I opened the door and called out, "Mom? Is that you?"

There was no answer.

Feeling a little nervous, I decided to check the entire house. I grabbed a can of aerosol hairspray in case I needed to spray some-one's eyes. (You can never be too careful!) Peering into the hallway, I stepped out. I checked each bedroom. The rooms were quiet and empty. I marched down the stairs. Next I scanned the kitchen and other rooms, noting where all the animals lay asleep in the sun streaming through a picture window. Finally I tested the locks on the front, side, and sliding glass doors.

I was the only person in the house.

Satisfied, I returned to the bathroom and closed the door behind me. As I turned to pull the shower curtain, I heard the stomping footsteps again. The sound was louder and more dis-tinct. There was no mistaking what I was hearing.

Now I felt a little scared.

I considered what to do next, ignoring the impulse to open the door and flee the bathroom. When the stomping occurred a third time, I whirled around and yanked the door open with a bang. I adopted my best irritated mom face and then stepped into the hall.

"All right, that's enough!"

I didn't hear footsteps again that day.

I've already addressed what the Bible teaches about spirits, life after death, and what I believe is the true identity of ghosts. The fact that similar experiences have been recorded for over two thousand years only leads me to believe that the harassing spirits who are the inspiration for these tales have no reason to change their MO.

If people will believe it and it's already established, why change what works?

I think it's important to know Christians are beginning to come forward with these kinds of personal stories. People tell me about their experiences because they know I'll listen and understand. In the past there has been an effort in the church to ignore anything that smacks of the paranormal or supernatural. This must change. I believe the church risks driving people to mediums or ghost hunters if it refuses to acknowledge what's going on around us.

This is why I counsel people on the reality of the spirit world and why I emphasize a Christian's authority in Jesus Christ.

Above all, we must be sure to keep everything in the proper perspective. The enemy is very subtle. He can lure us into shifting our focus from Scripture as our foundation. This is why the Bible must be what informs our faith and is used to "test the spirits" (1 John 4:1).

There was a time in my life when I was making judgments based on personal experiences alone rather than the truth of Scripture. I gave the weight of authority to what I felt or sensed, following the world's view of the supernatural and spirituality rather than God's.

Communicating with stories is a vital and important part of being human. I make room in my life for ancient myths, folk stories, fairy tales, and great works of literature—but I no longer indulge in modern horror books or movies. Why? I don't want to fill my mind with those images. There are so many avenues of temptation in the world, why add to my list?

I want my worldview to be shaped by Scripture.

I want to focus on serving God in this life and telling others about the good things He's done for me. I want to encourage people by telling stories of God's miraculous power in my life. I want to cheer people on in their faith.

Most ghost stories take place in the dark. I want to live my life in the light.

◂ ◂ DIGGING DEEPER ◂ ◂

Finally, brothers, whatever is true, whatever is noble, whatever is right, whatever is pure, whatever is lovely, whatever is admirable—if anything is excellent or praiseworthy—think about such things.
—PHILIPPIANS 4:8

1. Why do people like ghost stories?

2. Have you had any experiences you'd like to share with others?

3. Do you feel you can tell people at church about strange experiences?

4. Is there any potential harm in listening to or reading ghost stories?

5. Should the condition of our faith determine if we have enough discernment when it comes to ghost stories?

Chapter 15

MEDIUMS AND PSYCHICS

EING AWARE OF the spirit world is nothing new to me. I can't remember a time when I didn't sense spirit beings, both angelic or demonic—not all the time, mind you, but enough throughout my life to create recognition. As a Christian I have discernment as to whether or not various supernatural signs and wonders are from God.

When I walked away from the Lord, however, to become a witch, I was vulnerable to deception.

> The Spirit clearly says that in later times some will abandon the faith and follow deceiving spirits and things taught by demons. Such teachings come through hypocritical liars, whose consciences have been seared as with a hot iron. They forbid people to marry and order them to abstain from certain foods, which God created to be received with thanksgiving by those who believe and who know the truth.
> —1 TIMOTHY 4:1–3

Since reaffirming my faith, it has been interesting to observe the increasing popularity of mediums.[1] If the trend continues, I believe their celebrity will rival the spiritualist movement of the mid-nineteenth century. I recently learned of a psychic fair in 2010 that drew more than eight hundred people who were looking for readings from psychics and mediums.

How is this possible?

Take a look at the spirit communication industry. Television programs, books, seminars, and telephone networks abound. People are seeking comfort after the loss of a loved one or answers to life-impacting decisions. Mediums and psychics set up regular business hours at shops or have their own office spaces. Famous mediums are able to charge hundreds of dollars for a one-hour appointment. The average medium or psychic can charge thirty to sixty dollars per reading.

People will pay the cost.

A *medium* is a person with supernatural ability to engage in direct communication with spirit beings or the dead. A *psychic* is someone with similar abilities who can foresee the future or discern the past. They do not necessarily communicate with the dead.

Various classifications of a medium's ability have been created to understand the different ways in which mediums experience spirit communication:

- ✕ Full-trance mediums allow a spirit to temporarily possess their bodies and speak through them.

- ✕ Psychic mediums communicate mentally with spirit beings but remain in control of their bodies.

- ✕ Physical mediums experience or create manifestations outside of themselves but still within their environments as a result of their communication.

Examples of physical mediumship can include appearance of apparitions, direct voice (using a radio, TV, or electronic device), ectoplasm, levitation, materialization, rapping, or table tipping. A Ouija board or pendulums are considered examples of a physical medium's ability. Additional terms for people with psychic or mediumistic ability include sensitive, empath, intuitive, and channeler.

There are six major ways a medium or psychic's ability might manifest. Many psychics or mediums have one particular method of connecting to their supernatural senses, but most can experience a little from each category. These include:

× *Clairvoyance*—Clear seeing (perceive thoughts, images, or previously unknown information within the mind's eye)

× *Clairsentience*—Clear sensing/feeling (perceive thoughts, feelings, or previously unknown information through physical sensation or emotion)

× *Clairaudience*—Clear hearing (perceive sound otherwise not heard audibly)

× *Claircognizance*—Clear knowing (perceive information previously unknown)

× *Clairalience*—Clear smelling (perceive odors not detected by others)

× *Clairambience*—Clear tasting (perceive taste with nothing in the mouth)

Skeptics believe all medium or psychic ability is a fraud. People who set out to debunk this ability claim that mediums and psychics use cold readings (determining a person's body language using leading questions) to create the illusion of speaking with the dead, predicting the future, and so forth. In the case of physical mediums, skeptics declare nothing but outright trickery.

Not every person who claims to be a psychic or medium is honest. There are hundreds of scam artists who prey on the brokenhearted. But not every medium or psychic is a fraud. Experience proves to me the reality of spirit beings and paranormal phenomena. There are many who are in genuine contact with the spirit world. The problem is these psychics and mediums don't truly question what's behind the veil.

I am concerned for the mediums and psychics being influenced by spirits who mean them eternal harm. My heart aches for the people who unwittingly go to psychics and mediums for guidance or comfort. When I was a medium, I never bothered to question who the spirits interacting with me might actually be. I accepted everything I received from them as valid. After all, I only talked to "positive" spirit beings. I avoided anything that seemed negative or adverse.

I was primarily a clairsentient medium. I sensed spirits with my feelings or through sensations in my body. Over time I learned to communicate with spirit beings very effectively. I would receive detailed images, words, and phrases, or I would simply "know" the information they wanted me to convey.

Once I was with a friend and fellow ghost hunter who'd recently lost her mother. We hadn't seen each other for months before her mother's death. We didn't speak about her mother, other than my offering general sympathies. I'd never met my friend's mother or even seen a picture of her.

My friend and I were sitting in her car, chatting about work and other things when I sensed the presence of an older female beside me. The spirit being was very annoyed. I "knew" this woman was my friend's mother but was uncertain if I should mention anything to her. My friend's emotions were still raw, and she avoided talking about her loss.

"Just give her the pony" popped unbidden into my head. I had no idea what the phrase meant. The spirit being repeated the words, showing me a toy horse. I silently communicated that I didn't want to upset my friend with a message from her mother. The spirit being demanded my action by repeating the sentence over and over.

Finally I stopped my friend in the middle of her sentence. I hadn't heard a word she'd said anyway.

I told her about the invisible guest in the car, describing the "woman" beside me. "Your mother is saying, 'Just give her the pony.' She's showing me a toy horse. And she's being pretty surly about it. Does that mean anything to you?"

My friend stared at me for a moment before a small smile broke out over her face. She explained the meaning behind the odd declaration. She had been struggling with a decision about sending an antique toy metal horse from her mother's belongings to a young granddaughter. She worried the toy might be broken in transit or that the child was too young to receive such a gift. Laughing she said, "Well, all right. I guess I'll go ahead and send it."

I tell this story to make a point.

A spirit presenting itself as my friend's deceased mother gave me a message. Because we accepted this information as being legitimate, based on the accuracy of my reading, the advice was followed.

My question is this: How could we be sure this ghost was truly the spirit of my friend's deceased mother?

Simple answer—we couldn't!

There was—and is—no way to be certain. A deceptive spirit could have mimicked my friend's deceased mother. In fact, it is my firm belief that is exactly what happened. The "mother" provided me with enough information to appease doubt.

So why would a spirit being go to such lengths to try and prove the encounter was genuine?

The Bible provides us with the answer in the description of demonic spirits. By deceit and trickery they draw humans away from a true relationship with God.

My friend wasn't encouraged to seek God for comfort or guidance in her time of grief. Instead the experience encouraged seeking her "mother" for direction. I've witnessed a similar situation unfold in the lives of other people who communicated with "loved ones" through me as a medium.

Being a medium gave me a feeling of profound satisfaction. Every reading encouraged me to delve deeper. I honestly believed

I was helping people by connecting them with friends and family who'd died. Friends who discovered I was a medium wanted readings. People were impressed by how accurate I could be. One person teasingly called me a Jedi. I was told I'd been given a gift by God. What I didn't admit to myself were God's commands recorded in Scripture about people like me.

> Do not turn to mediums or seek out spiritists, for you will be defiled by them. I am the LORD your God.
> —LEVITICUS 19:31

> So do not listen to your prophets, your diviners, your interpreters of dreams, your mediums or your sorcerers who tell you, "You will not serve the king of Babylon."
> JEREMIAH 27:9

God did not want me to be a medium. Not ever!

My occult abilities were powered by spirits, twisting God's good gifts from their original intent—to serve Him and edify the church.

I'm grateful "there is now no condemnation for those who are in Christ Jesus" (Romans 8:1). Without that truth the enemy would have a field day torturing me over the people I inadvertently led astray as a medium. All I can do now is pray for anyone who received a reading from me. I can share the truth with those willing to listen.

Mediums and psychics can help no one. They and the people who have sought their advice have been lulled into a sense of peace by lying spirits. They are the blind leading the crippled, stumbling in the dark. Please don't make the mistake of following them into the abyss.

Jesus said, "Every plant not planted by my heavenly Father will be uprooted, so ignore them. They are blind guides leading the blind, and if one blind person guides another, they will both fall into a ditch" (Matthew 15:13–14, NLT).

◢ ◢ DIGGING DEEPER ◥ ◥

For the living know that they will die,
    but the dead know nothing;
they have no further reward,
    and even the memory of them is forgotten.
Their love, their hate
    and their jealousy have long since vanished;
never again will they have a part
    in anything that happens under the sun.
                        —ECCLESIASTES 9:5–6

1. Why are people interested in communicating with the dead?

2. Have you considered going to a medium? Why?

3. Why do you suppose God has forbidden the practice of mediumship or communicating with spirits?

4. Do you believe mediums are contacting the dead?

5. What can the church do to help people who are grieving?

Chapter 16

SPIRIT GUIDES

*W*HEN I FIRST began exploring the occult, I avoided the idea of personal spirit guides. As a witch I focused on psychic development. I dove into being clairsentient and the various means with which I could communicate with spirits. At the time I assumed the reticence was a holdover from church. Now I have a different opinion why I resisted spirit guides for so long.

What is a spirit guide?

Mediums and psychics claim that a *spirit guide* is an entity who chooses to remain disincarnate in order to act as a spiritual counselor or protector to the living. There are those who believe spirit guides can be angels, animals, or nature spirits. New Age proponents teach a spirit guide is your own higher wisdom or god within.

I was near the end of my journey when I decided to meet my spirit guides.

The Christian witch who served as my mentor mysteriously disappeared from my life. I was feeling the loss of her guidance and support. Even though she and I never agreed on my being a medium and ghost hunter, she encouraged me to make my own choices. As a Christian witch I prayed to God but relegated Him to the role of casual observer. I recognized Him as deity but not Lord. I called upon God during some of my spells, but otherwise I lived my life as I saw fit.

However, I still wanted someone I could turn to for direction.

When I made the decision to meet my spirit guides, I began

researching the best way to go about doing so. Meditation and visualization were the keys to success. The day I sought them out, I felt nervous. What if I was making a mistake? How could I be certain they knew what was best for me? Shoving the concern aside, I settled into a comfortable position on the floor and closed my eyes. Taking deep breaths, I centered my awareness within my mind. I relaxed into meditation, visualizing a white light shield of protection around me.

When I felt I was ready, I pictured a staircase in my mind's eye and began to climb. The trek was easy and relaxed, growing longer and longer as I climbed. I came to the top of the stairs into a wide garden of flowers spread out before me. There was a cobblestone path at my feet. I followed it until I reached a stone fence with an iron gate, which I now saw bordered the entire garden. There was an old-fashioned lock on the gate door. A park bench rested under a tree nearby. I felt in my pocket, and there was a key. I pushed the key into the lock and turned it. When I heard the loud snick of the lock being released, I reached out, twisted the handle, and pulled the gate open.

There was a dark void on the other side.

Suddenly I saw a man approach through the darkness. He came and stood in front of me. He wore a brown cowled robe. Inclining his head and sweeping his hand, the man beckoned me toward the bench. I allowed him to pass first and then followed, taking a seat beside him. The man introduced himself as Brother Marcus. He said he had been a monk in his former life and that he'd taken a keen interest in my life.

Brother Marcus was the first of five spirit guides who introduced themselves to me over the next few weeks. Each one had a different function in my life. There was a female spirit guide who gave me information during readings. Another claimed to have been a shaman before death. He came when I needed advice. I had a spirit guide who acted like an inner GPS. If I was lost, he would give me directions until I arrived at my destination. He gave me visions of a few ghost-hunting locations before I arrived for the investigation.

One spirit guide claimed to be Michael the archangel. He was my protector. After he told me this, I received validation of this claim during a ghost hunt. We were at an outdoor location. I was standing on one side of a narrow bridge, commanding a negative spirit to stay on the other side. It had been an active night. Many in our group had personal experiences such as being touched, feeling dizzy, or having a small object thrown at them. We'd grown accustomed to experiencing such occurrences during a spiritually active investigation. Hell's Bridge, a location we visited regularly, was no exception. When I felt the threat of the inhuman spirit had passed, I moved off the narrow iron bridge. The leader of the group photographed the entire event.

"Kristine, come here!" he demanded. He stared at the review screen of his digital camera.

I walked behind him, and peering over his shoulder, I saw the reason for his excitement. There was a picture of me standing on the edge of the bridge. A large orb was positioned in front of me.

"Yeah, that's Michael the archangel," I explained. "He's one of my spirit guides." I said this with absolute confidence. Why wouldn't I? Michael had told me he would be there.

When I became comfortable with the presence of these spirit guides, I couldn't imagine why I'd not wanted to meet them sooner. Whenever I needed assistance, they came to me. Soon, whenever I'd meditate, I'd go to the garden to visit with Brother Marcus. His presence was very soothing. And the more I opened myself to these spirit guides, the more accurate my readings as a medium became.

There was one drawback though.

I began to experience unwanted paranormal events in my home. Spirits began knocking on my bedroom windows while I meditated. Invisible hands tugged on my hair or touched my shoulder. Shadow people would move along the wall while I sat on the couch. I started creating a white light shield around the bed after my side of the mattress kept getting bumped while I tried to go to sleep.

One of my daughters heard footsteps at night. She glimpsed a "man" standing in the living room when she came downstairs for a drink of water. When she told me about it, I realized I'd witnessed a similar apparition a few nights earlier.

Needless to say, my daughter was deeply unsettled by the experience.

I asked my guides for help, upset that spiritual beings who sought my attention were becoming intrusive. I received no assistance or advice. My wise and benevolent spirit guides remained silent. I interpreted that to mean that the undesirable visitors were something I needed to get used to as a medium. I had to accept them as part of my life.

I never considered my spirit guides were the cause of the harassment.

When I used the key to unlock the gate to open the door to my spirit guides, what I did was give demons complete access to my life. I was fooled into believing these spirit guides were sent by God to direct me.

The night I repented, recommitting my life to Jesus Christ, it all came to a screeching halt.

My freedom was secured that very moment.

Every spirit I'd given permission to was compelled to obey the authority of my Savior and leave.

> And now you Gentiles have also heard the truth, the Good News that God saves you. And when you believed in Christ, he identified you as his own by giving you the Holy Spirit, whom he promised long ago.
>
> —EPHESIANS 1:13, NLT

Why do I believe I resisted spirit guides for so long? When I was a child, I accepted Jesus Christ, and though I was no longer following Him, the Holy Spirit never left me. Wherever I tried to run, He was there. The Holy Spirit prodded, reminded, and implored me through eight years of rebellion.

When I left the church all those years ago, turning my back on God, I thought it was because He'd abandoned me. Wrong!

I was the one who'd walked away.

I spent eight years searching for intimacy, and the One I was looking for was there all the time. The Holy Spirit is my comforter, teacher, and friend. He leads and protects me. He brings me up short when I need discipline. He strengthens my faith. He is training me in righteousness. He always points me to Jesus.

The Holy Spirit is the only guide I will ever need.

⤳ ⤳ DIGGING DEEPER ⤳ ⤳

Don't you realize that your body is the temple of the Holy
Spirit, who lives in you and was given to you by God? You do
not belong to yourself, for God bought you with a high price.
So you must honor God with your body.
            —1 CORINTHIANS 6:19–20, NLT

1. Do you know someone who claims to have a spirit
   guide?

2. Spirit guides are most often introduced and lead a
   person through subjective experiences of meditation.
   How does this contrast with being led or taught by
   the Holy Spirit?

3. Have you ever had an experience with a spirit
   guide(s)?

4. What do you believe is the overall purpose of spirit
   guides?

5. How should a Christian respond to spirit guides or
   someone who suggests incorporating spirit guides
   into Christian beliefs?

Chapter 17

WHEN DEMONS SCREAM

"WHAT WAS THE turning point?" I'm asked when I share my testimony. "What specific event brought you back to Christ?"

I used to hesitate before answering; this is where the story gets a little weird. I'm sure that sounds funny coming from me. Believe it or not, the turning point in my spiritual journey took place during one fateful ghost hunt.

Let me explain.

In 2007 I was a (mostly) content Christian witch and medium. I was a lead investigating member of a ghost-hunting group. We were receiving more requests for home investigations. I loved it. My abilities as a medium had grown to a place where friends encouraged me to charge a small fee for my services—not that I did. I never felt right about it. One woman held a reading party to showcase my talent, inviting neighbors she'd told about me. The woman served hors d'oeuvres and entertained her guests while I took those interested one at a time to a separate room for their reading. The evening was a great success. When I left, the woman was already planning the next event.

Life was very good.

My husband and I had successfully reunited after several previous attempts. He wasn't comfortable with the witch/medium/ghost-hunting thing, but he loved me. He wanted our family to be restored. This time he chose not to condemn or cajole me. Instead,

I later learned, he had started asking God to intervene and show me the truth.

Who knew the answer would be so literal?

My husband was in Georgia working on a consulting job when I got the call from my ghost-hunting team. We had an investigation right after Thanksgiving. I wasn't told any details, only where to go and when to be there.

When I arrived on location the next evening, I was told by a team member that the baseline reading of the house was running a little behind. I couldn't go in yet. Michigan winters can be very cold, so I decided to wait in the car with the heater running while preparing for my reading.

Centering myself, I started receiving information about the activity taking place in the house. My eyes were drawn to an upstairs window, but at the same time a need to check the basement was very strong.

Concentrating my attention on the window, I was surprised by the abrupt appearance of a young male spirit standing next to the car. He was leaning down, looking in through the driver's side window. He was agitated, insisting I should not go into the house. When he slammed his hand against the car window, I jumped. The intensity of the spirit's emotion was startling. He seemed to be afraid for me. Despite his protests I told him I had to go into the house.

When the team called me into the home, I walked through each room with a small digital recorder in my hand. One team member filmed my reading while another took photos with a digital camera. There were two primary spirits.

The one who came out to my car gave the impression of being a protector to the small children living in the home. The other was a hostile inhuman spirit. I no longer designated inhuman energy as angel or demon. I approached them as positive or negative by varying degrees. As I moved throughout the house during my reading, I was drawn to the children's bedroom on the second floor. The "young man" was now waiting for me there. In my mind's eye I saw him leaning over the youngest boy's bed, whispering words to him. I saw him sitting near the child on the floor, playing with small toys. When I moved to the basement, the area beneath the master bedroom and a playroom with a basket of toys held the strongest negative spirit energy. The words *child cater* came to my mind during the investigation. Later I learned the "friendly" entity did interact with the youngest son by speaking to him or moving small objects. The father reported the other entity had been harassing the children at night and in the basement play area. He appeared to them as a "dark man" and said scary things

After my reading of the house we set up the equipment for vigils in the designated hot spots.

Each member of the team had odd experiences that night. In the basement two of us saw a "red eye" manifestation as a set of beads fell off a box several feet from where we stood. The EMF detector lights shifted more than once in response to our questions. Temperatures fluctuated. We heard taps on the wall of the bedroom when we requested them.

As we moved to another section of the basement, I felt an overwhelming urge to tell the inhuman spirit to leave in Jesus's name. I hesitated. Sure, I knew about spiritual warfare from the church, but I hadn't done anything like that in years. Instead I used the Craft for exorcisms, which included smudging a room with sage while speaking a clearing incantation. Feeling awkward, I took a deep breath.

"In the name of Jesus, you are gonna leave," I mumbled. But as I spoke the words, confidence grew within me. "You're uninvited!"

My team gave me a strange look. Someone made a quiet joke; another person laughed. Nothing more happened from that point to the end of the investigation. We wrapped things up with a prayer for the home at the owner's request. Over the next several days two team members analyzed the recordings, video, and digital photographs for potential evidence.

Here is where the story gets interesting.

The team leader sent me an e-mail a few days after the investigation. "LISTEN TO THIS!" was the only message. He'd sent me a single audio clip. I downloaded the short file. Curious, I donned my headphones. Here I have to interject this, so you understand something: I've heard and seen some strange things in my life, especially after becoming a medium and ghost hunter. They include whispers recorded from verified empty rooms and unexplained mists, orbs, or apparitions caught on video or in photographs. I've heard voices, footsteps, breathing, taps. Lights and electronics have flickered as I've sensed spirit beings, with nothing in the mechanism, wiring, or batteries offering an obvious cause. I've been pushed when no one was behind me.

None of it comes close to what was on that audio file.

The clip starts as I'm telling the "inhuman spirit" to leave the house in the name of Jesus. On the audio clip you hear me saying, "You're uninvited!," after which the team leader quips, "You can't follow me home."

If you listen carefully, you can hear the laughter of my teammate. What took me by surprise was the angry, animal-like shriek and loud thump over the top of it.

Stunned, I listened to the audio clip again.

A demon had been forced to leave at the name of Jesus Christ.

I'd read about such things in the Bible—Paul commanding the unclean spirit to leave the slave girl. I'd witnessed spiritual warfare as a teenager when the pastor commanded that demon to leave my room. But now I was actually hearing it happen!

A little freaked out, I forwarded the e-mail to my husband. As a professional audio engineer, I figured he would have the necessary expertise and computer programs to test the clip. I wanted to know if my teammates were winding me up because of the

"Jesus thing." I needed to be certain that what I was hearing on the audio file was a genuine EVP. I asked him to analyze it for me.

My husband called a few days later. We chatted for a while about his current job, our daughters, and other typical life stuff. I told him I missed him, and he assured me he'd be home in a few weeks. I waited for him to say something about the EVP. When he didn't, I decided to broach the topic.

"So, did you get that e-mail I sent you with the audio file?" I asked nervously.

"Yep. I don't know what it is, but it's real. What have you been doing?"

He listened as I recounted the entire story.

"Well, like I said," my husband remarked, "nobody faked that audio."

Hanging up the phone, I walked over to the computer and sat down. I put the headphones over my ears and brought the audio file back up. Chills ran down my spine as I listened to it again. Taking a deep breath, I removed the headphones and placed them on the desk. Standing, I walked up the stairs and into my bedroom and closed the door behind me. I moved to the closet. Looking up at the shelf I could see the one Bible I'd kept after turning to Wicca eight years prior. I reached up and grabbed it. The Bible was a weight in my hands. I hugged it to my chest for a moment as I sat down on the bed. And then I opened it.

I read these words:

> What did your ancestors find wrong with me that led them to stray so far from me? They worshiped worthless idols, only to become worthless themselves.
> —JEREMIAH 2:5, NLT

My heart broke. Did I make God feel that way when I turned to the goddess? Did He feel abandoned when I invited spirits to give me guidance? But they were sent to help me *by Him*, weren't they?

I spent the next day reading every scripture I could find on witch-craft, mediums, psychics, and the occult. I reacquainted myself with Jesus as the Bible describes Him, not the version I'd created.

I kept thinking about the EVP. I'd listen to it and cringe.

> They will spread out their bones on the ground before the sun, moon, and stars—the gods my people have loved, served, and worshiped. Their bones will not be gathered up again or buried but will be scattered on the ground like manure.
>   —JEREMIAH 8:2, NLT

> They exchanged the truth of God for a lie, and worshiped and served created things rather than the Creator—who is forever praised. Amen.
>   —ROMANS 1:25

The presence of the Holy Spirit was heavy on me. A dark spiri-tual veil was yanked from over my head. My eyes filled with tears. I had been as foolish and blind as a Christian could be. I've heard people call Jesus a psychic and a magician. There are a few brave souls who claim Him as a witch. They are wrong.

Jesus is the Son of God.

> Your eye is a lamp that provides light for your body. When your eye is good, your whole body is filled with light. But when your eye is bad, your whole body is filled with dark-ness. And if the light you think you have is actually darkness, how deep that darkness is!
>   —MATTHEW 6:22–23, NLT

These are the words that broke me. I got down on my face and repented of everything. Praying for hours, I wept, confessed, and rebuked the demons I'd allowed into my life. God's mercy and grace delivered me that night, and I've been thanking Him every day since.

I'm not offering the "Demon Scream EVP" as proof of anything. I share my story to illustrate how God opened my eyes to the truth. The Holy Spirit reaches out to each of us differently. I have no idea why God used a ghost hunt and EVP to knock me up side the head. Maybe He knew it was the one thing that would get my attention in the end.

During an interview I was asked what the power of Jesus means to me. The answer is so simple:

Healing. Salvation. Love.

Jesus is everything.

⸙ ⸙ DIGGING DEEPER ⸙ ⸙

You believe that there is one God. Good! Even the demons believe that—and shudder.

—JAMES 2:19

1. What does the power of Jesus mean to you?

2. Jesus gives us His authority as disciples. How do you define that in your life?

3. Do you think Christians take Jesus's power seriously?

4. Are you ever afraid to pray or speak in the name of Jesus? Why?

5. Do you believe a spirit can return after it is commanded to leave? Why or why not?

Chapter 18

DELIVER ME FROM EVIL

TWO YEARS AFTER reaffirming my faith in Christ, I began experiencing spiritual backlash.

Out of nowhere I longed for the familiar acquaintance of ritual and magick. Old habits reasserted themselves in my thoughts and behavior. I searched the Internet for witchcraft sites. I joined and left message boards. One day while browsing through a bookstore, I snuck over to the metaphysical section. I found myself picking through sets of tarot cards, fighting the desire to purchase one. Every night the moon beckoned me. And when I'd go to the front door, a presence was there, coaxing me to give it entrance.

This went on for months. I didn't tell anyone. My husband and I had recently found a small church to attend. We volunteered when needed. I signed up to go on a mission trip to Costa Rica. My husband and I made an effort to get to know people, but I still felt alienated. Every day I asked God to bind and remove the spirits oppressing me. I'd read 2 Corinthians 5:17: "Therefore, if anyone is in Christ, he is a new creation; the old has gone, the new has come!"

I'd gain relief, but the struggle would return a few days later.

As the mission trip drew near, I began to have serious doubts about going. Since childhood one of my dreams was to be a missionary. The idea of going to another country and helping people in God's name still pulls on my heart. All the details had been set. The trip cost was covered. I had my passport. It was my spirit that was troubled.

Was I a hypocrite? How could I minister to people when I was so weak myself? I realized it was long past time to talk to my husband.

"Listen," I told him as I lay my head on his shoulder, "I've been having a hard time lately."

My husband pulled me into a gentle hug as his arm wrapped around me.

"What's going on?"

I confessed everything to him. He wanted to know why I hadn't said anything. What caused the temptation in the first place? I honestly didn't know. Was there anything he could do to help? I asked him to pray for me. When I voiced my concerns about going on the mission trip, he put them to rest with assurances that nobody in ministry is perfect.

"You should go," he admonished.

When I arrived on the ground in Costa Rica a week later, I knew I'd made the right decision. God was answering a prayer from my childhood. I had no idea He would also choose to answer my most recent ones.

I was part of a large group from my church. We were joined by two other groups. We were divided into small teams for the various tasks set by the host church. We met at the main building for breakfast and devotions in the morning. Our translators and team leader told us our assignment for the day. We'd climb aboard a bus or van for transport. The weather was hot, and we worked hard—painting, building, cleaning. We were brought back to the host church for lunch before returning to finish our tasks or projects. In the evening our large group would meet for dinner one last time before we were transported to host homes.

Midweek provided an opportunity for us to clean up after dinner and attend the church for a service with our host congregation. Seated among the people, we sang familiar praise and worship songs in Spanish. The language barrier became nonexistent as we were hugged and received by these brothers and sisters in Christ. The head pastor gave a message, which was translated for us. As he finished, the front stage area was opened for people to come forward for prayer. The pastor made a point of inviting the Americans as well. People were moving from their metal folding chairs to the front.

The Holy Spirit urged me to join them.

I felt rooted to the spot. My breath caught for a moment. Why was I resisting? What was I afraid would happen? Did I truly want the enemy to bend me into submission once more? Suddenly I was moving around the chairs, finding a space in which I could stand. I didn't wait for the prayer team to find me.

Time stood still as I talked to God.

Gentle hands touched my shoulders as women surrounded me with prayer. I heard their voices, English and Spanish, but couldn't follow their words. My own whispered broken prayer continued to pour out. The women moved on, but I couldn't leave. God wasn't finished with me yet.

My eyes were closed, so I didn't see her approach.

A woman who'd come to serve with us for the week was in front of me. I'd shared my testimony with her and a few other people at lunch the day before. I didn't mention the difficulties I'd been experiencing the past months. Her hands came to rest on both sides of my face. She spoke softly as she leaned her forehead into mine. There were tears in her voice as she told me the Holy Spirit wanted her to pray about my occult past.

God was going to finish the work.

I have no idea how long she prayed for me. She joined my renunciation of the past and rejoiced in the ministry she believed God was preparing for me. I began sobbing and trembling when she rebuked the enemy who was tormenting me. As her prayer flowed over me, I saw God's angels grab those demons, hurling them away.

Finally the woman pulled me into a tight hug. Both our faces were washed of any makeup we'd bothered to wear that evening. Pulling back, she smiled. I returned it as God's peace filled me.

"I can see the light of Christ in your eyes," she declared. "Never forget you are free."

Even when she left, I had to stay with those few still remaining. Now my prayer was filled with grateful thanks. One of the leaders from our church appeared by my side, asking if I was all right. Nodding, I assured her everything was fine. When the worship team returned to the stage to play a few more songs, I went to find my seat.

The enemy wanted me to feel captured by my past, isolated from brothers and sisters in Christ, never admitting I am vulnerable to sin. Why? The enemy has this game all set up so that even as a Christian I can be chained by my flesh. What can I do about it?

Change the rules of the game.

So this is me, being real. No masks. I'm not perfect. Never have been or can be. There are times I'm still tempted by former interests in the occult. There are days, weeks, or even months I get spiritually sideswiped and need my husband or the church to lift me up. Sometimes my faith is so tiny it's hard to remember I have any.

You know what else?

Jesus has given me the authority of His name. My weakness is His strength. All things are possible for me in Christ. There is nothing in this world or the next that can keep God's love from me. The only chains on my wrists are the ones I put there.

I'm still learning how to be genuine in my daily walk. I'm discovering how to live in a community of believers again. When I seek out others to join me in prayer, I see the walls of opposition come crashing down, but it can take time. As I notice the whispers of the enemy, I tell him who I am.

Spiritual oppression will occur. Temptation happens. These are facts of the Christian life.

How I respond is what matters in the end.

✐ ✐ DIGGING DEEPER ✐ ✐

I have discovered this principle of life—that when I want to do what is right, I inevitably do what is wrong. I love God's law with all my heart. But there is another power within me that is at war with my mind. This power makes me a slave to the sin that is still within me. Oh, what a miserable person I am! Who will free me from this life that is dominated by sin and death? Thank God! The answer is in Jesus Christ our Lord. So you see how it is: In my mind I really want to obey God's law, but because of my sinful nature I am a slave to sin.

—ROMANS 7:21–25, NLT

1. Do you ever feel pulled down by temptation?

2. Are you able to go to a Christian to ask for help if you are faltering in your walk? Why or why not?

3. Is there any temptation you believe other Christians won't understand?

4. Have you ever experienced spiritual oppression?

5. Are there Christians who never struggle with their faith?

A SPECIAL PRAYER FOR DELIVERANCE

Holy Lord,

I stand before You in humility, my soul laid bare by the regrets of my past. There are things I've done that could drown me in shame if the enemy were allowed. But I know You, Lord. You are merciful, God. You are quick to forgive. Your love knows know boundaries. I belong to You.

Break the chains that bind me to the sins of my past. They are over, no longer in Your sight. Let the blood of Jesus, which cleanses me from all sin, wash me clean. Throw off any remnant of the enemy from my back. Strengthen me to withstand temptation or attacks of the evil one. I stake my claim on holy ground as Your servant. I stand with feet firmly planted on the authority YOU have given me through Jesus Christ. Remove any blight or stain, ungodly influence, and unclean spirit from me. Deliver me, O God, from my enemy. And hold me in Your righteous hand.

In Jesus's name, amen.

PART 3

WHERE DO WE GO FROM HERE?

Do not fear, for I am with you; do not anxiously look about you, for I am your God. I will strengthen you, surely I will help you, surely I will uphold you with My righteous right hand.

< ISAIAH 41:10, NAS >

Chapter 19

GIVE ME A SPOTTER'S GUIDE!

*H*OW DO YOU recognize someone who is practicing witchcraft or is interested in the occult?"

I get asked this question a lot, and I have a difficult time providing the desired answer. People want a list of visual cues, a spotter's guide to the occult. I can't give more than vague generalizations.

The question doesn't address the real issue.

There is no way to know a person's heart or mind through simple observation. People will cite clothing style, crystals, or other objects as potential clues. Only wearing black, enjoying candles, and having a naturalist's taste in décor does not signify occult interests. Unless you find books with the word *witchcraft* in the title or recognize pagan symbols in artwork on the wall, everything is up for interpretation.

Take me for example. I'm an average-looking woman. There is nothing about my appearance that suggests my religious beliefs. I don't go for stereotypes. My clothes are modest but modern. I wear earth tones as well as bold colors. My nails might be painted black, pink, or brown. My jewelry is eclectic. Nothing about how I look or decorate my home screams "CHRISTIAN!"

Bet you wouldn't have pegged me as a witch either.

Not wanting a firestorm of reactions from Christian family or friends, I remained hidden. My sacred space was dual purposed for decoration. My necklaces were either a triquetra (the Celtic trinity symbol claimed by pagans and Christians) or a quartz crystal pendant. There are people who wear paganism on their sleeve, but not as many as you might think. Most of the witches I knew kept their beliefs private unless they were asked.

Because of this I've learned to pay attention to what people say. Does a person's conversation suggest she struggles with her faith? Has she pulled back from participating in activities with other Christians? Does she speak well about the church in general? Is she willing to talk about Jesus? The answers may point to a spiritual crisis.

When I immersed myself in occult thinking, my heart hardened toward traditional Christian teaching. I knew how to sound Christian. But my actions spoke the loudest. I stopped singing on the praise team or going to home group. My speech became peppered with phrases such as "I sense..." When I stopped attending church, few people missed me. Not surprising, as I'd made myself invisible by merely warming a pew. Those who did reach out I pushed away with misplaced anger. I surrounded myself with like-minded individuals who reinforced my beliefs as a witch, medium, and ghost hunter.

There were some Christian family and friends to whom I told the truth. Here is what they did.

They dug deeper and weren't afraid of my spiritual beliefs. I never felt judged by their questions. During these conversations they never told me to have more faith. We talked about sin and what that means. We talked about relationship with God. When they had their own crisis of faith, they were honest about it. They talked about what Jesus had done for them.

They accepted me and trusted me to God's hand.

Often I think people want a *spotter's guide* so they can be sure that their loved ones find repentance with as little fuss as possible. The desire is driven by love, but such motives also involve fear. I'm a control freak, so I understand the motivation. God is the one who pokes at the spirit for necessary change. Our job is to be willing to notice.

✦ ✦ DIGGING DEEPER ✦ ✦

Do not judge by appearances, but judge with right judgment.
—JOHN 7:24, ESV

1. How should a Christian define *right judgment*?

2. When can a Christian judge a brother or sister? Why?

3. Why is it important for Christians to hold one another accountable?

4. When you meet someone (Christian or otherwise), how often do you make up your mind about that person based on his or her appearance?

5. Why do we need to focus on what other people are saying?

Chapter 20

How Should Christians Respond?

FTER I SHARED my testimony at a church, a man stood up during the Q and A session and suggested that Christians should have nothing to do with people who practice witchcraft. He believed Satan's hold over them was too strong, so that even sharing the gospel would be a dangerous endeavor.

I was brought up short by that comment.

When the man finished speaking, I pointed out that as disciples of Jesus Christ we are meant to share the gospel with everyone. Who they are, where they've been, or what they have done should never be a factor when telling people about God's love and grace.

Sadly I've heard the suggestion to avoid witches or pagans expressed in the church more than once. Christians who endorse befriending people of other major religions will stridently avoid anyone involved in the occult. There are some who refuse to talk about anything related to witchcraft. People seem to fear spirits will be given free rein over hapless Christians who dare broach the subject.

I've encountered a similar attitude toward people who experience paranormal phenomena. No one in the church is willing to talk to them or offer guidance on how to deal with these situations biblically. As a result Christians are turning to psychics, mediums, and ghost hunters for answers. What they learn eventually becomes melded into their beliefs.

I've been asking the Holy Spirit for wisdom on these issues.

What came to mind was a deeper study of Paul's visit to Athens. Out came my Bible. I read Acts 17:16–34 (ESV), taking time to read the verses carefully and study the commentary.

As I read the account, I was struck by Paul's response to the idols throughout the city. He was troubled (burdened) by what he saw. He had a deep concern to share the good news of Jesus Christ with the Athenians. Therefore Paul went into the marketplace where he reasoned with the Jews and devout people he found there. He conversed with the philosophers and was invited to present his teaching at the Areopagus (Mars Hill).

The bottom line throughout the exchange was Paul's attitude.

Paul made his case citing the Athenians as a deeply religious people. Pointing out an idol dedicated "To the unknown god," he proceeded to introduce them to God.

> He is the God who made the world and everything in it. Since he is Lord of heaven and earth, he doesn't live in man-made temples, and human hands can't serve his needs—for he has no needs. He himself gives life and breath to everything, and he satisfies every need. From one man he created all the nations throughout the whole earth. He decided beforehand when they should rise and fall, and he determined their boundaries.
>
> His purpose was for the nations to seek after God and perhaps feel their way toward him and find him—though he is not far from any one of us. For in him we live and move and exist. As some of your own poets have said, "We are his offspring." And since this is true, we shouldn't think of God as an idol designed by craftsmen from gold or silver or stone.
>
> God overlooked people's ignorance about these things in earlier times, but now he commands everyone everywhere to repent of their sins and turn to him. For he has set a day for judging the world with justice by the man he has appointed, and he proved to everyone who this is by raising him from the dead.
>
> —ACTS 17:24–31, NLT

Some of the people scoffed, others were interested and wanted to learn more, and a few became believers in Jesus Christ that day. Paul never wavered from addressing the sin of idolatry. He got his point across without insulting his listeners or belittling their current beliefs. He confidently pointed them to God while paying attention to his surroundings. He persuaded people with the truth.

Paul understood when to drive home a point and when to leave the debate. I've taken a tip or two from Paul when it comes to talking to Wiccans, witches, and pagans. I can share the truth that God is reaching out in love to every single one of them. Those listening may choose to believe or not, but that is their decision.

> For though I am free and belong to no man, I have made myself a slave to everyone, to win as many as possible. To the Jews I became like a Jew, to win the Jews. To those under the law I became like one under the law (though I myself am not under the law), so as to win those under the law. To those not having the law I became like one not having the law (though I am not free from God's law but am under Christ's law), so as to win those not having the law. To the weak I became weak, to win the weak. I have become all things to all people so that by all possible means I might save some. I do all this for the sake of the gospel, that I may share in its blessings.
> —1 CORINTHIANS 9:19–23

Paul was an effective evangelist because he understood his freedom in Christ. He was able to discern the needs of the people around him without compromising the truth. Can you imagine the reaction if we start living in the freedom that Jesus Christ provides—a relationship without fear? Some people will still get offended by the gospel, but it will be on them. There will be others who will listen and want to know more. There will be the few who say yes to Jesus.

We live in an era where paganism is making a comeback. Wicca is one of the fastest-growing religions in North America.[1] Today's Wiccans, witches, and pagans aren't all that different from the people Paul addressed on Mars Hill.

If we will look past the witchcraft to the person, we will find someone whom God loves. In the same way we can adopt Paul's attitude when dealing with those interested in or experiencing the paranormal. We can share Scripture, stand with people in prayer, and never compromise the truth.

How to Help Someone Deal With the Paranormal

I talk to a lot of Christians who believe they've experienced some kind of paranormal event. There are others who have a friend who claims to have seen a ghost. Many are fearful. They want to understand why God would allow them to experience such weird stuff in the first place. These people want to know what they can do as Christians to deal with the paranormal.

Step One: Check what the Bible says.

Don't assume something odd is happening in your life or a friend's because of demon activity. We all deal with temptation, sin, and the consequences of our actions. There is the possibility God may be stirring up our lives to help us grow and mature in our faith.

Step Two: Listen to a person's story without jumping to conclusions.

Many so-called paranormal events have a very down-to-earth explanation. Be willing to consider environmental factors and equipment malfunction. Is a door that seems to open on its own actually on loose hinges? Could flickering lights be faulty wiring? Are shadow people or apparitions created by cars' headlights reflecting off windows? Examine pictures or video given to you carefully. Nine times out of ten, anomalies can be explained by dust, bugs, lens flare, and glare.

Take into account any drinking, medication, depression, stress, or illness at the time of the experience. Are the details exaggerated? Do they sound more like horror movie special effects than a typical ghost sighting or haunting?

Use common sense in judging a person's story (or your own experience) to determine if a legitimate paranormal event has occurred. If you are encountering a supernatural situation, deal with it through spiritual warfare prayer. The situation may resolve immediately. When dealing with oppression, there could be a longer process involved. Spiritually sensitive people should be ready to stand firm through prayer, fasting, and asking mature Christians for support.

> This is why I remind you to fan into flames the spiritual gift God gave you when I laid my hands on you. For God has not given us a spirit of fear and timidity, but of power, love, and self-discipline.
> —2 TIMOTHY 1:6–7, NLT

The most important thing for any Christian is to be grounded in Scripture. Meditate on the spiritual armor God provides us (Ephesians 6:10–18): the helmet of salvation, shield of faith, belt of truth, shoes of peace, and sword of the Spirit. Wear your armor daily.

The man I mentioned at the beginning of this chapter did have a point. The enemy does have his power invested in witchcraft and paranormal activity. The same is true with anything in this fallen world, which is why it's important to be in a right relationship with God. This has proven to be true no matter whom the Lord brings across my path.

So I keep short accounts with Him, confessing when I mess up. I press into my relationship with Jesus Christ. I trust the leading of the Holy Spirit. Isn't that what Paul did? This is how we respond as Christians living in a troubled world.

We reach out with faith, hope, and love.

✦ ✦ Digging Deeper ✦ ✦

There is no fear in love, but perfect love casts out fear. For fear has to do with punishment, and whoever fears has not been perfected in love.

—1 John 4:18, ESV

1. What do you know or believe about witches, Wiccans, and pagans?

2. Should a Christian befriend a witch or pagan? Why or why not?

3. Why do you think the church ignores topics like witchcraft or the paranormal?

4. Do you know anyone who claims to have seen a ghost? How did you respond to his or her story?

5. Would it affect your faith if you had a paranormal encounter?

Chapter 21

SPIRITUAL GIFTS

$\mathcal{B}$ECAUSE I DO not shy away from topics that involve the supernatural, I am often asked about spiritual gifts. There seems to be confusion among churchgoers today—some are firm in their understanding, while others are confused. The most common concern is that spiritual gifts and occult abilities are similar. How do we tell the difference? Here is what we know.

We serve a supernatural God.

He is awesome in power and authority. Through the Holy Spirit He empowers us as Christians to share the good news of the gospel, care for others, and encourage one another in the faith. He also gives each of us spiritual gifts according to His purpose to be used for His glory.[1]

Our enemy is supernatural as well, one who likes to counterfeit the good things of God. The enemy is "the father of lies" (John 8:44). He was thrown down from heaven for his pride. He dared to believe he could be like God (Isaiah 14:12–14; Ezekiel 28:12–19; Mark 3:22; Luke 10:18; Revelation 9:1). This was how Lucifer became Satan (the adversary), the old serpent, the devil, and Beelzebub. Now the enemy spreads confusion in the world, but the Bible teaches that God has overcome his schemes.

However, the enemy's defeat hasn't stopped his attempt at mimicking God's power.

The Old Testament shows us how God communicated with His people through visitation, revelation, dreams, and inspiration. The angel of the Lord appeared to individuals such as Abraham,

Hagar, Jacob, Moses, and Joshua (Genesis 22:11–18; 16:9–10; 32; Exodus 3:2–5; Joshua 5:13–15). He was present in the burning bush and the pillars of fire or smoke. The Holy Spirit would anoint or cover people for specific purposes.

Who were the ones chosen by God to speak or act in His name? Normal people going about their daily lives for whom God had a purpose, not unlike you and me. There were fifty-eight known prophets (forty-eight men, seven women) recorded in the Old Testament. The four big guns were Isaiah, Jeremiah, Ezekiel, and Daniel.

There were also plenty of false prophets in the land. In all likelihood they outnumbered the real ones. They were anyone who claimed to be speaking for God but weren't actually hearing from Him. Sure, they were listening to "something" (the enemy, their own voice) and convincing others to believe them. They sweetened their words with everything the people wanted to hear. And, you know, I'm positive they thought they were doing God's will. I think they were sincere in their beliefs.

Never mind that God hadn't actually uttered a word to them.

In the New Testament we learn that God revealed Himself through the ministry, death, and resurrection of Jesus. When Jesus ascended to heaven, the Holy Spirit was released to dwell within every person who accepts Christ as Lord. As a result how we hear from God has adjusted to accommodate His constant presence in our lives.

This is how God interacts with the world through the church today.

> In the past God spoke to our forefathers through the prophets at many times and in various ways, but in these last days he has spoken to us by his Son, whom he appointed heir of all things, and through whom he made the universe.
> —Hebrews 1:1–2

Consequently, you are no longer foreigners and aliens, but fellow citizens with God's people and members of his household, built on the foundation of the apostles and prophets, with Christ Jesus himself as the chief cornerstone. In him the whole building is joined together and rises to become a holy temple in the Lord. And in him you too are being built together to become a dwelling in which God lives by his Spirit.

—EPHESIANS 2:19–22

But everyone who prophesies speaks to men for their strengthening, encouragement and comfort. He who speaks in a tongue edifies himself, but he who prophesies edifies the church.

—1 CORINTHIANS 14:3–4

God works directly through His people by gifts of leadership, administration, helping, teaching, encouragement, wisdom, healing, faith, knowledge, discernment of spirits, prophecy, and tongues. When submitted to Christ, these gifts allow God to do amazing things through believers. I've been a witness to it.

Do you remember my trip to Costa Rica? Let me share another story with you from that week.

First, you need to know about the small church we were working with in Palmares. The congregation had ministered in the area for less than ten years at that time. Their buildings were located in the poorest, most densely populated section of the city. Unemployment and alcoholism were rampant. Most of the congregation (three hundred people) walked or found a ride to attend worship. The church reached out to the surrounding community through multiple ministries, including skills training for machine repair and sewing. They were being salt and light, proclaiming the gospel, and the enemy noticed. The doors of their worship center were chained and locked by local authorities six times over the years. Yet the people of this church had bold faith.

Healings—physical, emotional, and spiritual—were taking place. The lost were coming to Christ. Marriages were being restored.

Near the end of the week my group with our interpreters went on a walk through several neighborhoods of Palmares. We were charged with two tasks: invite couples to a special free showing of the movie *Fireproof* (babysitting provided), and pray for people. Whatever their need, we were going to lift it up to God—ask for help in finances, healing, whatever. It was near the end of July. The weather was supposed to be rainy but was unseasonably dry and hot. The water was absent throughout the entire city that day. As we walked into the heart of the neighborhood, the smell of raw sewage was a strange juxtaposition to the lush green plants and brightly colored flowers lining the broken sidewalks.

Our interpreters led us up to each dwelling, where they shouted a greeting in Spanish. They explained the purpose of our visit. Most residents smiled, observing the Americans with pleasant interest. When we offered to pray for their needs, the majority shook their heads before retreating inside.

A few said yes.

Two women invited our walking party into their home. As the older woman spoke, the interpreters shared her concerns for jobs for their husbands and food for the children. She moved to stand in the center as we placed our hands on her shoulders to pray as God led. While we prayed, the Holy Spirit nudged me. I peeked up at the younger woman and suddenly realized she was pregnant.

"Tell her the baby is a blessing. I have plans for the child. Pray for them both."

My companions finished their prayer and started to ready themselves to leave, saying good-bye to the inhabitants. I leaned toward one of the interpreters and asked if I could pray for the younger woman. After gaining her permission and drawing my companions back, I placed my hands on the woman's shoulders. Looking into her eyes, I repeated what the Lord instructed me to say. As I began praying, she closed her eyes and started weeping. By the time I finished, we were all crying. The woman looked at me then pulled me into a tight hug. Through the interpreter she said she'd been asking God for days why He'd cursed her with another child. She felt overwhelmed. God had responded to her prayers in a way she never expected.

Both women accepted Jesus Christ as their Savior before we left the house that afternoon.

Some may ask how that was different from what might have happened when I was a medium. There are many differences. I was part of a group of faithful Christians submitted to God in prayer. The presence of the Lord surrounded us. The words put on my heart to share with the woman honored Him. The saving grace of God was the final result—an eternal result.

As a medium I offered people hollow comfort, drawing them to communicate with their dead loved ones or other spirits. God wasn't honored. Vanity was the end result, because the enemy provided the counterfeit.

A Christian gifted by the Holy Spirit will never offer a message that contradicts God's truth as revealed through Scripture. This doesn't mean we can't be fooled by the enemy or by our own desires if we aren't careful. For this reason we are admonished not to believe everything we hear simply because it sounds good.

> Beloved, do not believe every spirit, but test the spirits to see whether they are from God, for many false prophets have gone out into the world. By this you know the Spirit of God: every spirit that confesses that Jesus Christ has come in the flesh is from God, and every spirit that does not confess Jesus is not from God. This is the spirit of the antichrist, which you heard was coming and now is in the world already.
> —1 John 4:1–3, esv

Many psychics and mediums receive messages from spirits who draw people to look within themselves for answers to life and the universe.

Even in the church there are those who claim to be speaking for God, but the spirit behind their words is false. They may not say outright, "Jesus didn't come in the flesh," but it's implied in the result—people are filled with doubt about God, Jesus is seen as a good teacher but not the Savior of the world, and the message of the church (and therefore Jesus) is flawed because everybody should "win."

The enemy is clever. He works through subjective human emotion to spiritually deceive. We see this evidenced in the temptation of Jesus in the desert:

> Then Jesus, full of the Holy Spirit, returned from the Jordan River. He was led by the Spirit in the wilderness, where he was tempted by the devil for forty days. Jesus ate nothing all that time and became very hungry. Then the devil said to him, "If you are the Son of God, tell this stone to become a loaf of bread."
>
> But Jesus told him, "No! The Scriptures say, 'People do not live by bread alone.'" Then the devil took him up and revealed to him all the kingdoms of the world in a moment of time. "I will give you the glory of these kingdoms and authority over them," the devil said, "because they are mine to give to anyone I please. I will give it all to you if you will worship me."
>
> Jesus replied, "The Scriptures say, 'You must worship the LORD your God and serve only him.'" Then the devil took him to Jerusalem, to the highest point of the Temple, and said, "If you are the Son of God, jump off! For the Scriptures say, 'He will order his angels to protect and guard you. And they will hold you up with their hands so you won't even hurt your foot on a stone.'"
>
> Jesus responded, "The Scriptures also say, 'You must

not test the LORD your God.'" When the devil had finished
tempting Jesus, he left him until the next opportunity came.
—LUKE 4:1–13, NLT

What did the enemy use to tempt Jesus? Carnal desires (food),
power, and acknowledgment. His tactics haven't changed. Did you
notice the enemy twisted Scripture to his own purpose? We must
be able to discern when God's Word is being used improperly, as
Jesus demonstrated in His retort. The same principle applies to
things we hear and see that are attributed to God.

God's interaction with us should never be confused with the
practices of paganism.

I've learned to be careful about adopting a mentality that spiritual gifts are something to be practiced or achieved. Words of
knowledge, prophecy, and interpretations of tongues or dreams
are meant to edify the church. I believe God gifts His people
according to His purpose and glory as it's needed. Spiritual gifts
are not taught, honed, or crafted as I did with my occult abilities.

God's spiritual gifts are received.

> It is the one and only Spirit who distributes all these gifts.
> He alone decides which gift each person should have.
> —1 CORINTHIANS 12:11, NLT

I don't seek out signs and wonders. Instead I wait for God's
leading. Moving from one spectacle to the next, trying to acquire
something the Bible calls a gift, is demanding my will not His.
My focus narrows to what I think best. I want to avoid the error
of the Pharisees in Matthew 12:38–45 who requested a miracle
affirming Jesus's authority.

God has nothing to prove to me.

⸙ ⸙ DIGGING DEEPER ⸙ ⸙

Now concerning spiritual gifts, brothers, I do not want you to be uninformed. You know that when you were pagans you were led astray to mute idols, however you were led. Therefore I want you to understand that no one speaking in the Spirit of God ever says "Jesus is accursed!" and no one can say "Jesus is Lord" except in the Holy Spirit.

Now there are varieties of gifts, but the same Spirit; and there are varieties of service, but the same Lord; and there are varieties of activities, but it is the same God who empowers them all in everyone. To each is given the manifestation of the Spirit for the common good. For to one is given through the Spirit the utterance of wisdom, and to another the utterance of knowledge according to the same Spirit, to another faith by the same Spirit, to another gifts of healing by the one Spirit, to another the working of miracles, to another prophecy, to another the ability to distinguish between spirits, to another various kinds of tongues, to another the interpretation of tongues. All these are empowered by one and the same Spirit, who apportions to each one individually as he wills.

—1 CORINTHIANS 12:1–11, ESV

1. Do you believe the Holy Spirit works in the church through spiritual gifts? Why or why not?

2. Have you experienced one or more of the gifts? Which one(s)?

3. How was God glorified through spiritual gifts?

4. Do you believe Satan mimics God's spiritual gifts? How? Why?

5. Which spiritual gifts seem most effective in reaching the unchurched?

Chapter 22

THE DANGERS OF DABBLING

*H*AVE YOU EVER thought about the word *dabble*? Dictionary.com defines it as: "to work at anything in an irregular or superficial manner."[1] In other words, it may be of interest for a while, but it doesn't necessarily become a passion.

People can dabble in many different things—baking, cooking, literature, gardening, yoga, dance, writing, sports, auto mechanics, woodworking, jewelry making...you name it. Any discipline or skill that can be learned has the potential to be *dabbled* in.

There is some risk when it comes to dabbling. For instance, if you merely dabble in various activities, you could become a "jack of all trades but master of none"—never focusing enough so as to become proficient at any given task. This can be useful in some situations, but it can also prove to be a liability when doing a job that requires specific skills.

When I was in college, I had this nice little car for getting around town. Unfortunately I never bothered to learn proper maintenance of the car. My school was in Florida, so the car stayed on campus throughout the year. My mother took care of getting tune-ups and oil changes when I came home in the summer. The only thing I did was drive the thing. One day the engine began knocking and sputtering. A friend told me he knew all about cars and would take a look. He lifted the hood and gave the engine a cursory overview. My friend determined the car needed oil. He drove me in his own vehicle to the gas station, instructing me on the type of oil I should purchase and how much was needed.

When we returned to campus, he went to my car and began filling it. Six quarts of oil later during a test drive the engine seized.

He'd put in too much oil.

My friend thought he knew enough about cars to diagnose the problem. The truth is, he dabbled in auto mechanics. He had a working knowledge of engines but not enough necessary information to repair them.

The damage to my car was irreparable. I learned two valuable lessons from it all. The first was the necessity of becoming a responsible adult. The second was this: there are situations where dabbling can lead to a dangerous outcome.

The occult falls into this category. I've discovered many people will ghost hunt, play with Ouija boards, or indulge in some other occult activity with little understanding of it. Many are drawn to horoscopes without realizing they are connected to astrology. Professed Christians will play with Angel Oracle cards unaware it is no different than the tarot. What's sad is that the people who are dabbling have no idea they are even doing so.

Let's take a look at magickal correspondences as an example.

Crystals and gemstones have traditions or symbolism that surrounds them from ancient days. We all know diamonds are associated with romance, marriage, wealth, and longevity. Did you also know that the diamond's energy corresponds with the elements of air and fire? The sun is its planetary connection. Diamonds can be used in spell casting to address infertility and sexual dysfunction. They are effective in rituals for scrying, astral travel, meditation, or enhancing intuition.

Now, I'm not suggesting anyone throw away his or her diamond jewelry. I wear an anniversary ring with emeralds because it symbolizes that my husband and I have passed the twenty-year mark of our marriage. We can acknowledge tradition or symbolism without fear. But there is additional information available that you should know. The purpose? Prudence and awareness.

Occultism is hidden in many corners of society, including the jewelry counter. How does it affect you? If you want that amethyst necklace because it's pretty or uniquely designed, I'm right there with you. If you want the necklace because the neat little card suggests it's good for depression, stress relief, or mental acuity, you need to think twice. Those descriptions are referencing energy correspondences.

I'll put it in a nutshell: wearing amethyst because it can sharpen your thoughts is dabbling in gemstone magick.

I'm convinced that Christians should be aware of mystical beliefs attached to things in our culture. We don't need to be paranoid or ensnared by overt interest, but we should recognize the occult when we see it. At the very least, a red flag should raise in our thoughts when confronted by mysticism. This reminds me of Jesus's words to the disciples as He sent them out in pairs to minister. "Look, I am sending you out as sheep among wolves. So be as shrewd as snakes and harmless as doves" (Matthew 10:16, NLT).

Most of the time people who play around in the occult have some notion of what they are doing. However, once a spiritual door is opened, it can be difficult to shut in the long run. The results can be loss of faith, depression, obsession, addiction, and relationship trouble.

> Abstain from every form of evil.
> —1 THESSALONIANS 5:22, ESV

God is looking out for our best interests when telling us to stay away from divination, mediums, false prophets, witchcraft, sorcery, and every form of the occult. If we decide to ignore His warning and indulge an interest, we open ourselves to being hurt. Certainly there are situations where we stumble into something unknowingly. The important part comes when it's time to act. As truth is revealed—do we walk away or sneak back to it once in a while? My first experiences with occultism were formed through testing the waters. Ultimately I was pulled in.

The truth is that when we mess with things we shouldn't, there are inevitable consequences. Dabbling feeds into temptation, becoming sin in the end.

✦ ✦ DIGGING DEEPER ✦ ✦

No temptation has overtaken you that is not common to man. God is faithful, and he will not let you be tempted beyond your ability, but with the temptation he will also provide the way of escape, that you may be able to endure it.
—1 CORINTHIANS 10:13, ESV

1. Have you ever been tempted to dabble in the occult?

2. How does God provide a way of escape for you?

3. Do you believe things like horoscopes are harmful? Why or why not?

4. What other things in society have occult meaning?

5. How do you avoid "every form of evil"?

Chapter 23

WHAT ABOUT HARRY POTTER?

I HAD JUST FINISHED speaking before a large group of Christian women.

Tipping the live microphone down to my side, I reached out with the other hand for a cup sitting on the table behind me. I took a sip of water as the event hostess stood up. Gesturing to the women, she asked if anyone had a question for me. Hands shot up all over the audience. I pointed to a lady in the back. Even as she stood, I knew what she was going to ask.

"What do you think about Harry Potter?"

Truth be told, I dread that particular question.

It's a loaded one. Most of the time the person asking already has a strong viewpoint and is looking to me for validation. Regardless of my answer, the topic often dissolves into a protracted discussion.

Being a former witch, I understand why people want my opinion about Harry Potter. I'm just not sure adding another voice to the argument is going to do anything to bridge the gap this divisive issue has caused among Christians.

For the record, I have no personal issue with the author, the stories, or the movies created from the Harry Potter series. I have read all of the books. I've seen every movie. My view is that Harry Potter is similar to any story featuring the battle between good and evil. As the characters mature over time, we see all the ups and downs of life. In the struggle for Harry's survival the reader is witness to every foible of humanity.

Do the stories contain references to real practices in the occult? Yes.

There are several forms of divination, conjuring, ghosts, mythical creatures, and various uses of witchcraft. I think it's important to be aware such references are present. The story takes place in a world separate from normal humanity. In Harry Potter a witch or wizard is born with its powers. There is no way for an ordinary person to be a part of the wizarding world. Most of the magic displayed in Harry Potter is typical fantasy-type stuff.

Will reading the Harry Potter books cause a child to be drawn toward the occult as he or she grows older? I can't deny that it's possible. The real issue, to me, is whether an interest exists before reading the books or seeing the movies. Truthfully, the average reader or moviegoer will probably never be enticed toward witchcraft because of Harry Potter.

However, there will always be some kids or adults who are drawn to magick regardless. If my father was an alcoholic, I will decide not to touch alcohol—because it will fuel temptation. Likewise, if a child has a leaning toward the occult, why read Harry Potter, which will only further awaken that desire?

So with that said, it begs to be asked: Would witches and ghosts have interested me if I hadn't heard stories about them in my childhood? The answer is yes, I would have turned to the supernatural anyway. Yes, popular media played its part, but I would have found a way to explore witchcraft eventually.

Communication is key when it comes to Harry Potter.

The Harry Potter phenomenon can be an excellent opportunity to talk with youth about matters of faith. Discussions can range from the nature of good and evil, sin, sacrifice, mercy, forgiveness, loyalty, jealousy, lying, consequences for our actions, and more. All are themes that occur throughout the series. Because they reference true occult practices, these stories can be a catalyst for discussions on the reality of the spiritual world. Talk about the difference between fantasy and occult magick. Discuss what the Bible says about witchcraft. Topics such as death and grief can also be addressed through situations in the books and by discovering how the Scriptures respond.

One important point.

If you're not planning on reading or viewing alongside your children, then don't let them read the books or watch the movies. Kids don't have a clue how to deal with some of the emotional issues presented in these stories. The Harry Potter series takes place over seven years. The plot becomes spiritually heavy as Harry and his companions mature. Terrible situations and painful feelings are explored. Young people should not be left to navigate these scenarios on their own.

The Harry Potter books and movies have come to an end. There's no denying the series left its mark on the entertainment industry. Over the years its influence and popularity have encouraged more books on the market that cater to interests in the occult or supernatural. Ignoring the trend would be counterproductive to dealing with it as a Christian.

I believe it's important to seek God's guidance on how to respond with wisdom and grace.

There is an adage attributed to P. T. Barnum, which says: "All publicity is good publicity." We may never know if the contentious debate within the Christian community regarding Harry Potter might have actually contributed to its overall success and longevity, but it's something to bear in mind.

⸌⸌DIGGING DEEPER⸍⸍

Don't have anything to do with foolish and stupid arguments, because you know they produce quarrels.

—2 TIMOTHY 2:23

1. Have you read the Harry Potter books or watched the movies?

2. What did you learn about witchcraft or the occult from Harry Potter?

3. Why do you think Christians have been divided over Harry Potter?

4. How do you define a foolish argument?

5. Is there anything valuable to learn from fantasy books or stories? Why or why not?

Chapter 24

THE TWILIGHT SAGA

HE FIRST TIME I heard about a book called *Twilight*, I didn't understand all the fuss. When the details of the story were explained to me, I realized the plot is not exactly original. Yet somehow the Twilight Saga series has captured the imagination of millions. The near hysteria that young girls, teens, and women have expressed toward this story absolutely floored me.

I decided to investigate *Twilight* for myself.

What I found is a series of books and movies filled with occult or supernatural themes and imagery.

The story follows the life of a girl named Bella Swan. In *Twilight* Bella has moved to a new town and is contemplating a boring life when she encounters the mysterious Edward. Soon they fall headlong into a passionate, forbidden romance. Throughout the story Bella is swept into a series of events that take a deadly turn and threaten everyone she knows. I have to admit on the surface the story sounds pretty interesting.

Did I happen to mention Edward is a vampire? A vile, blood-drinking demon who brings death in his wake?

Well, that's what Edward would be if his character was true to his folktale origins.

Vampires are said to be beings that steal the life-force (energy or blood) from the living. Belief in demons who ate flesh and drank blood can be found in ancient cultures such as the Mesopotamian, Hebrew, Greek, and Roman. Modern superstitions surrounding vampires come from Romania and Southeastern Europe. This is where we get familiar traditions such as garlic as a repellent and a wooden stake through the heart. The traditional personification of a vampire as alluring was introduced in John Polidon's *The Vampyre* (1819). The image would become permanent through Bram Stoker's *Dracula* (1897).

The important point is that vampires were always evil.

I've heard people use this as an argument against *Twilight*. This makes sense, since so much of the story is based on occult themes and characters. My personal opinion is there is a deeper issue, and that issue is the reason I warn people to consider the Twilight Saga very carefully. The series is not, as devotees will proclaim, an epic romance.

Twilight is a story of dangerous obsession.[1]

Bella Swan, the heroine, is not a sympathetic character. I can hear the objections already, but that's how I read her. She's selfish, manipulative, and has no appreciation for the (living) people who care for her. She even rejects a more suitable love interest. (Yes, I know. Jacob is a werewolf, but Mike isn't!) Instead Bella is fixated on the dangerous-looking boy who has seemingly shunned her. She desires what seems unattainable. She doesn't understand the first thing about honest relationships or love. Later in the series Bella forsakes her soul so she can be with Edward forever. How is that healthy?

And what about Edward?

He was initially attracted to Bella because her blood held particular appeal to his vampire senses. When she was around, he avoided her. Edward wasn't being noble. She was a potential snack, and he feared being caught by the authorities! Pure and simple, he was stalking her as any predator would with an instinct to kill— not exactly the basis for a good relationship. Edward overcame his desire to eat her by becoming infatuated with Bella's humanity. Edward is a sensual creature. What he feels for Bella is lust fueled by selfish desire. He does grow to care for Bella, but if Edward truly loved the girl, he would walk away from her. He doesn't.

This is why I find the Twilight stories so disturbing. They glorify everything love is not, drawing impressionable young women into an unhealthy expectation of intimacy and romance.

Obsession occurs when a person becomes emotionally fixated on someone else. This is a kind of codependency that can lead to harmful relationships. The first signs of obsessive love include an immediate move from attraction to romantic involvement within the early moments of meeting. There is an urge to rush into immediate relationship regardless of potential character flaws, dissimilar interests, or concerns from family.

These obsession elements are woven into the story line and character motivations of the Twilight Saga. Bella is immediately drawn to Edward despite his apparent attempts to push her away. When she learns of his true nature as a vampire, her desire for him increases. Edward sneaks into Bella's bedroom at night to watch her sleep before they are a couple. When Edward leaves Bella to protect her from his enemies (evil vampires), she becomes reckless and suicidal. Bella is insistent on becoming a vampire despite Edward's seemingly selfless objections. She eventually gets her way.

The list goes on.

When I think of love, relationship, and what it means to be in covenant marriage with my husband, I turn to the Bible for a definition.

> Love is patient, love is kind. It does not envy, it does not boast, it is not proud. It is not rude, it is not self-seeking, it is not easily angered, it keeps no record of wrongs. Love does not delight in evil but rejoices with the truth. It always protects, always trusts, always hopes, always perseveres.
> —1 CORINTHIANS 13:4–6

Real love is always rooted in God.

I challenge you to take an objective look at what the Bible describes as love. My husband and I have worked very hard to maintain a relationship for over twenty-three years. We have been able to do so, despite a five-year separation, in large part to a renewed understanding of friendship, love, and covenant. Speaking from that experience, I don't believe Bella and Edward (their actions, motivations, declarations) can ever demonstrate an honest, romantic relationship. As a mother I wouldn't want my daughters involved in any kind of situation that mimics Bella and Edward's story.

Young women reading the Twilight Saga are swept into an epic tale that skews perception of genuine affection or tenderness. They become caught in the emotional wake of the characters. In the end readers will have dabbled in Bella and Edward's obsession expecting to find a similar love of their own. As parents we need to encourage our children to seek a covenant with their future spouse as God intends.

I'm told there are redeeming values to the Twilight Saga. I will concede that may be true. If women and teen groups are discussing the difference between obsession and love using the Twilight Saga as a resource, I applaud their resourcefulness.

But I fear everyone is too busy choosing Team Edward or Team Jacob to bother.

⤙⤙ DIGGING DEEPER ⤚⤚

For this reason a man will leave his father and mother and be united to his wife, and the two will become one flesh. This is a profound mystery—but I am talking about Christ and the church. However, each one of you also must love his wife as he loves himself, and the wife must respect her husband.

—EPHESIANS 5:31–33

1. Have you read the Twilight Saga or watched the movies?

2. Do you believe Edward and Bella emulate these verses? Why or why not?

3. How do you define *obsession*? How do you define *love*?

4. What is the difference between a promise and a covenant?

5. What do you believe is the central theme of *Twilight*?

Chapter 25

SCARY MOVIES

*I*N OCTOBER 2009 my husband forwarded an e mail he thought I might find interesting. Included was a short news article and a web address for a movie called *Paranormal Activity*. The article detailed a remarkable outpouring of support for the movie. The Internet campaign was so popular that more than one million people cast a vote requesting the movie be released to theaters nationwide.

Let me share a little background. *Paranormal Activity* was a low-budget, independent project originally filmed in 2007. It was put on the shelf to languish for two years. Through the clever use of the Internet over six months and limited screen releases, *Paranormal Activity* suddenly became a hot commodity.

Everyone talked about the film. Top critics declared it one of the scariest movies in recent years. Once the film made it into nationwide release, *Paranormal Activity* became one of the most profitable movies ever made.

Paranormal Activity's plot revolves around a young couple named Katie and Micah. Life had apparently been moving along successfully enough for them to move in together. We learn early on that the peace of their home has been disturbed by an invisible presence coming to them every night as they sleep.

The main target of the disturbances is Katie. As the movie progresses, we learn she has experienced paranormal activity from the time she was a child, such as remembering seeing a black shadow figure at the foot of her bed.

Attempting to deal with the situation, Micah purchases an expensive camera with the intention of videotaping their room at night. He hopes to capture evidence of their experience so he can determine the nature of the activity and devise an action plan. The movie switches between footage of the couple during the day to the nighttime footage. As viewers we are witness not only to the supernatural events occurring in the home but also to the slow deterioration of the couple's relationship. The strain and fear of the increasing intensity of events takes its toll.

The movie is presented in much the same manner as *The Blair Witch Project* (1999). An opening screen shot introduces the film as genuine footage discovered by authorities. The film is spliced together with date stamps to offer a time line of events. This cinematic strategy brings a sense of reality to the viewer and makes the movie seem all that more frightening. The bulk of paranormal activity occurs off screen, building tension as each day progresses. It's a very clever way of filming. Let's face it; what you don't see is more frightening.

When I first wrote about *Paranormal Activity* for *Kristine ReMixed* in October 2009, I had watched a few of the promotional clips. There was a time when I was a huge fan of horror films. In college I joined a group of friends in what we called "The Gore Corp." If there was a fright fest in the theater, we went to see it. Stephen King was my favorite author. Now I try to stay away from scary stuff. Horror films and books leave me feeling unsettled in my spirit.

I wasn't planning to watch *Paranormal Activity*—ever.

What changed my mind? The questions generated by my article about the film. People wanted to know more. Did the movie portray a haunting from a realistic viewpoint? What was my opinion of horror movies in general? Should Christians go to see *Paranormal Activity*?

A year later people were still asking the same questions. The release of the DVD brought the movie back into public thought. When *Paranormal Activity 2* (and later the third installment) was produced, even more people wanted to know what I thought about it.

I needed to see *Paranormal Activity*.

Decision made, I went to the nearest video store, rented the DVD, and brought it home. Since I wasn't sure if the fright factor lived up to its stated reputation, I watched the movie in the full light of day. My dog was at my feet; a pen and notepad were in my hand.

Considering the low budget spent on the film (something like $15,000), I was pleasantly surprised when the quality was better than expected. Sure, it was rather like watching home movies, but it was a relief to know I wasn't going to endure a stylistic shaky mess. The main characters, Katie and Micah, were interesting and had a chemistry that worked as though they really were a loving couple.

I confess I was impressed by the realistic nature of the paranormal events being experienced by the couple. Most of the action in the film was accurate to a haunting people have reported. It was similar to what I have witnessed, heard, or felt in my life or through my former activities as a medium and ghost hunter. The exceptions were some spontaneous combustion and the final fifteen minutes, which were typical Hollywood shock.

The paranormal activities represented in the film were loud footsteps, breathing, phantom drafts, whispered voices, taps or bangs on walls and floors, items being moved, doors being opened and closed, movement of the bed or sheet on the bed, shadow people, lights or electronics turning on and off, and recorded electronic voice phenomena.

Some of what's listed can be explained by natural occurrences in the environment, (creaking houses, noisy plumbing, loose hinges, faulty wiring). But if those are eliminated, then its possible real phenomena could happen as depicted.

I did appreciate that the creator of the film didn't try to make the story about a ghost. The haunting spirit was identified as a demon. Traditional references to ghosts were made several times, which makes sense considering the subject matter.

Sadly, Katie consults a psychic, and Micah brings a Ouija board into the home in an attempt to deal with their problem. The redeeming feature of the decision is being shown what not to do. Their actions serve to make matters worse, propelling the story to its ultimate tragic conclusion.

In my opinion *Paranormal Activity* accurately depicts the addictive nature inherent in paranormal investigation. The more evidence Micah obtains using the video camera, conducting EVP experiments, and using the Ouija board, the more he wants to continue. He even gets to a point of challenging the demon to show itself. Micah's obsession creates friction between him and Katie. She simply wants it all to stop. By the time Micah realizes he's in over his head, it's already too late.

Here is the big question. Should Christians watch the movie *Paranormal Activity* (or its sequels)? What about other horror films or books?

As with anything of this nature, every person needs to make his or her own decision as God leads. I didn't find the movie very scary. The clip I previewed on the Internet in October 2009 left me feeling disturbed, but I had no spiritual check as I watched the DVD. If it had been dark or I'd been in a theater with a hundred nervous people, who knows? I certainly didn't have trouble going to sleep that night. Nothing weird began happening in my home as a result of watching *Paranormal Activity*.

What I take into account when deciding if I should watch a movie, television program, or read a book factors down to this:

Will it make me stumble in my walk with Christ?

What about people around me?

> You say, "I am allowed to do anything"—but not everything
> is good for you. You say, "I am allowed to do anything"—but
> not everything is beneficial. Don't be concerned for your
> own good but for the good of others.
>
> —1 CORINTHIANS 10:23–24, NLT

There is nothing inherently wrong with watching scary movies. We are not condemned by reading a horror novel. But what are those images doing to our minds and hearts? Are we allowing the enemy to have a foothold of fear in our lives? Are we accepting cultural explanations for the spiritual world over what Scripture teaches?

These are things I have to take into consideration when making a decision like this.

The problem with a movie like *Paranormal Activity* is how realistic it is. It's very easy to suspend disbelief and accept the premise of the story as fact. When books and films blur the line of reality and illusion, it's time to consider opting out of the experience.

> Finally, brothers, whatever is true, whatever is noble, whatever is right, whatever is pure, whatever is lovely, whatever is admirable—if anything is excellent or praiseworthy—think about such things. Whatever you have learned or received or heard from me, or seen in me—put it into practice. And the God of peace will be with you.
>
> —PHILIPPIANS 4:8–9

↗↗ DIGGING DEEPER ↘↘

Think about the things of heaven, not the things of earth.
—COLOSSIANS 3:2, NLT

1. What do you think about scary movies?

2. Have you seen any of the *Paranormal Activity* movies? Why or why not?

3. Is there any harm in reading a horror novel?

4. What does it mean to renew our mind in Christ?

5. How do you define thinking about things of heaven and not earth?

Chapter 26

THE ORIGINS OF HALLOWEEN

OCTOBER IN MICHIGAN is a beautiful time of year. There is a chill in the air as leaves turn from lush green to bright red and brown. Orange pumpkins make an appearance on front lawns, street corners, and in grocery store displays. Fresh apple cider and plain cake doughnuts become staple pantry items. The smell of autumn is in the air.

I look forward to it every year.

When I was a child, October heralded more than a reminder of autumn's golden harvest. For me it was a time of spooky fun. I spent the entire month drawing black cats, reading ghost stories, and planning what I would be for Halloween. The day was an event. On the morning of October 31 I'd shove my (usually homemade) costume into a paper grocery sack. The bus ride to school was filled with animated discussions and critiques of our holiday attire. Half of the day was devoted to decorating the classroom, changing clothes, and marching in a parade. In the afternoon my mother and I would carve a smiling jack-o'-lantern from a large pumpkin. Time would drag until finally it was six o'clock!

The real Halloween fun could begin.

I'd bang out the front door, swinging a plastic bucket through the air. Skipping down our long driveway, I'd hurry across the quiet country road to my friend's house. I'd be greeted at the door by a clown, princess, or whatever character she chose to become that year. We'd acknowledge her mother's advice to be careful with a wave, hopping down the steps and crossing the yard. There were no cars as we danced up the road in the hastening dark. We'd approach the door of each house with a shouted "Trick or treat!"

I was a high school student the first time I heard that some Christians don't celebrate Halloween.

I was no longer an age to beg for candy from my neighbors, so I volunteered to help my church with a party of local kids. Sometime during the night the youth group leader and his wife stopped in to speak with the pastor. Their children, I noted, were not in costume or playing any of the games. When I asked why, the youth group leader told me they didn't allow their kids to celebrate Halloween because the day represented Satan. At the time I didn't really understand their position.[1]

Years later, when my own children were small, I remembered that conversation.

By then more churches were beginning to offer harvest festivals or alternatives to Halloween. So my husband and I dressed our daughters as Bible characters and took them to church parties. I still carved a pumpkin. We'd use stars, hearts, and crosses to make them into luminaries in place of a jack-o'-lantern.

As a witch I returned to the celebrations of my youth. I'd purchase or make costumes for my girls and bring them to my sister's suburban neighborhood for trick-or-treating. The pumpkins turned back into jack-o'-lanterns. For several years I dressed up and went to Halloween parties hosted by friends.

Near the end of the night I would retire to my own room for a private ritual. I'd cast a sacred circle. A white candle would be in the center in remembrance of my ancestors. I'd use a pendulum made of orange carnelian or pull out my deck of tarot cards with vintage Halloween images for future-casting. Time was spent in quiet reflection on my goals for the new year. If I had a pressing need, a spell was cast.

Since returning to Christ, my husband and I view Halloween as a time to reach out to children and parents with the light of the gospel. We often volunteer at our church for ministry opportunities to the surrounding community. When I open my door to trick-or-treaters, a pocket-size Gospel of John is included with the candy.

Because I'm a former witch, many Christians ask my opinion about Halloween. What are its origins? Is it OK for Christian kids to trick-or-treat? Should the church ignore it or repurpose the day into an outreach?

These are legitimate questions.

Many Christians are uncomfortable with Halloween because of the darkness of its roots. Halloween is one of the few festivals that has maintained the nature of its traditions. But with the current popularity of the holiday, it can be hard to avoid the trappings associated with it as you go to the store, library, or school.

Halloween finds it origins in an ancient Celtic fire festival observed more than two thousand years ago in Ireland. It was known as *Samhain* (pronounced "sow-in" or "sow-een"), which translates, "Summer's End." The Celts divided their year into two seasons: summer and winter. October 30 was the last day of the old half of the year (summer), and November 1 was the first day of the new (winter).

October 31—Samhain—was a time between.

A "time between times" was considered by the ancient Celtic Druids to be sacred and magickal. It was a brief window when the veil between the physical and spiritual realms was thin. The Celts believed that during this "time between," the dead walked among the living. Elemental spirits roamed the land. Festivals, feasts, and sacred rites were held on this day that included communicating with the dead, divining the future, animal sacrifice, wearing masks to hide from evil spirits, relighting hearth fires in preparation for winter, and leaving out scraps of food for wandering souls.

Many Christians have been led to believe this fire festival was dedicated to a lord of death known as Samana or Samhain. There is a problem with this assertion; no such lord of death existed in Celtic lore. Their gods of the underworld included Gwyn ap Nudd (Welsh), Labraid (Welsh), and Arawn (Irish). The October 31 Summer's End celebration did not revolve around any particular god. The error apparently originated with Colonel Charles Vallency in the 1700s in a series of books he wrote about the Druids, which still persists.

By A.D. 43 the Romans had conquered most of the Celtic lands. Similar festivals and customs from both cultures were intermingled among the citizens. When Constantine declared Christianity the religion of the empire, the church's influence began to spread across the known world. The church attempted to incorporate the festivals people still observed into Christian tradition. As a result November 1 was introduced as *All Hallow's Day*, a time to honor Christians who had passed the previous year. The *Summer's End* festival became known as *All Hallow's Eve*. During the Middle Ages the title was shortened to *All Hallow's Een*.

Time would see October 31 become known as *Halloween*.

Modern Halloween traditions have medieval origins rather than a direct connection to ancient Druid rites. Trick-or-treating can be traced back to an English All Soul's Day tradition (which falls on the day after All Hallows), where the poor went to wealthy homes to receive soul cakes in return for a promise to pray for deceased relatives.

The celebration of Halloween was introduced to America by Irish immigrants in the 1800s. Familiar symbols of the holiday were adapted from their stories and traditions. For instance, the carving of a jack-o'-lantern. An Irish legend tells of Stingy Jack. He had a bad habit of making deals with the devil and then tricking him. After Stingy Jack died, he was denied entrance into heaven by God because he was such an unsavory character. The devil wouldn't let him into hell. Stingy Jack was doomed to walk the earth with nothing but a glowing coal placed inside a carved turnip he used as a lantern. Irish Americans discovered pumpkins were more plentiful than turnips, and the jack-o'-lantern we know today was created.

Do children face increased danger on Halloween? No more so than any other day of the year. While there is no doubt the symbolism of October 31 is centered around death and spooky things, most people consider it a fun, secular holiday—a day devoted to playing dress up and eating candy. Common sense should dictate where and how parents allow children to participate (if at all) and what kind of parties they should attend.

Trick-or-treaters being targeted for harm on Halloween is nothing more than an urban legend.

There are rumors claiming human or animal sacrifices occur on Halloween. If such activities exist, they fall in the realm of self-styled Satanism (not to be confused with the legal religion created by Anton LaVey, Theistic Satanism, Wicca, or traditional witchcraft). Stories of human sacrifice on Halloween are based on urban myths originating from the satanic panic of the 1980s. I'm not saying such crimes never occur, but it's not as typical as some Christians seem to believe.

Wiccans and witches do celebrate Samhain as a holy day. They use the time to reflect upon the previous year and honor the dead. October 31 is still considered a time of great power. Wiccans and witches hold rituals and feasts as part of their Samhain celebrations.

Is there a greater risk that children will be influenced by witchcraft at this time? The answer is no. Wiccans and witches are focused on their own spiritual beliefs, families, and traditions on Halloween. Worries such as these are based on hype, not reality. This kind of fear forgets the awesome power of God, who is our shield and strength.

Should Christians celebrate Halloween?

I can't answer that question for you. As Christians we need to follow the leading of the Holy Spirit in this and all matters. People who choose to allow their children to trick-or-treat, carve a pumpkin, or throw a costume party should do so without condemnation.

The same holds true for those who do not participate in Halloween activities. Families can go to an alternative event such as a harvest celebration or All Hallow's Eve service. Some may choose to spend the evening in prayer for the lost or volunteer their time toward a worthy cause.

We are encouraged not to dwell on darkness but shine the light of Christ for the whole world to see. We are commanded to concentrate on what it is good, pure, holy, and righteous. We are also reminded that we become all things to all people in order that they may hear the gospel and be saved.

Whatever your convictions about Halloween, the most important thing to remember is not to be overcome by fear. You always have the assurance of "he who is in you is greater than he who is in the world" (1 John 4:4, ESV).

⚬ ⚬ DIGGING DEEPER ⚬ ⚬

And whatever you do or say, do it as a representative of the
Lord Jesus, giving thanks through him to God the Father.
—COLOSSIANS 3:17, NLT

1. Do you believe Christians should celebrate
   Halloween? Why or why not?

2. Should the church have brought pagan festivals into
   Christian tradition?

3. What other Christian holidays have borrowed from
   pagan customs?

4. How do you spend your time on October 31?

Chapter 27

SPIRITUAL WARFARE

*S*OME DAYS I forget I live in a spiritual battlefield.

I'm going about my life, not thinking beyond the moment; everything around me is status quo. And then it happens—the car stops working, money is in short supply, a job is lost, people I once thought were friends turn their backs. In short, I'm blindsided by difficult circumstances in a narrow window of time. Murphy's Law seems to be using me as a test case. I'm left wondering what happened as I deal with the emotional or financial fallout.

We live in a broken world, so bad stuff happens. There are consequences for actions. What I'm talking about is different. It usually comes on the heels of a blessing from God. The Holy Spirit has issued a call, and you've responded with faith. A prayer is answered after years of patient waiting. It's during these times that temptation rears its head. The enemy challenges our maturity.

A spiritual battle wages around us every day. The enemy knows he's lost but is determined to exert as much influence in this world as possible. Satan seeks to steal, kill, and destroy all that God loves. As a result we are caught in the cross fire.

> For though we live in the world, we do not wage war as the world does. The weapons we fight with are not the weapons of the world. On the contrary, they have divine power to demolish strongholds.
>
> —2 CORINTHIANS 10:3–4

> Be self-controlled and alert. Your enemy the devil prowls around like a roaring lion looking for someone to devour. Resist him, standing firm in the faith, because you know that your brothers throughout the world are undergoing the same kind of sufferings.
>
> —1 PETER 5:8–9

The good news is God has provided us with everything we need to be successful in the battle. He empowers us to overcome the enemy and his schemes. In Ephesians 6:13–18, Scripture offers us a description of the spiritual armor that serves to protect and equip us. The weapons of our warfare are grounded in daily obedience to God and the authority of Jesus.

When I'm feeling particularly challenged by the enemy, there's one piece of that armor I claim every day—the belt of truth. I meditate on how wearing it affects my life. I ask the Holy Spirit to help me remember to put it on so I can be prepared.

> Therefore, put on every piece of God's armor so you will be able to resist the enemy in the time of evil. Then after the battle you will still be standing firm. Stand your ground, putting on the belt of truth and the body armor of God's righteousness. For shoes, put on the peace that comes from the Good News so that you will be fully prepared. In addition to all of these, hold up the shield of faith to stop the fiery arrows of the devil. Put on salvation as your helmet, and take the sword of the Spirit, which is the word of God. Pray in the Spirit at all times and on every occasion. Stay alert and be persistent in your prayers for all Christians everywhere.
>
> —EPHESIANS 6:13–18, NLT

Here is what I've learned while putting on my spiritual armor:

- *The belt of truth*: Jesus is the way, truth, and life.
  There is no condemnation in Christ. I am held by

the truth of the gospel no matter how difficult life
might be.

- *The helmet of salvation*: I can bring every thought
  into captivity.

- *The breastplate of righteousness*: I am called to a holy
  life, honoring God in all I do and living according to
  His purpose. Christ covers my heart. In imitating
  Him, I can make each day count by loving God and
  people.

- *Feet fitted with the readiness of the gospel*: I am called
  to proclaim the truth of Christ and share His love
  and the peace that good news brings. Love God; love
  people. My feet stand on the peace of God's saving
  grace.

- *Shield of faith*: I'm to walk in faith, trusting God's
  grace and standing firm against the tricks and
  temptations of the enemy.

- *Sword of the Spirit*: The Word of God tells me everything I need to know about my Savior and myself.
  The Holy Spirit uses Scripture to teach and guide me
  along the way.

There are those today who deny the existence of Satan. Their
unwillingness to acknowledge the spiritual world is of little consequence to reality. I'm honestly not surprised. The Bible reveals:

> First of all, you must understand that in the last days scoffers
> will come, scoffing and following their own evil desires. They
> will say, "Where is this 'coming' he promised? Ever since our
> fathers died, everything goes on as it has since the begin-
> ning of creation." But they deliberately forget that long ago

by God's word the heavens existed and the earth was formed
out of water and by water.

—2 PETER 3:3–5

So what do we do? How do we move forward in this spiritual
battle?

- Seek God in everything.

- Test all spirits, man-made traditions, and doctrines
  you hear.

- Be certain what you learn matches the Word of God.

- Talk to God every day.

- Pray for family, friends, the church, and those in
  your sphere of influence.

- Invest yourself in relationships with mature
  Christians.

- Maintain a proper perspective of who the enemy is
  while remembering God is over all.

Look, I have given you authority over all the power of the
enemy, and you can walk among snakes and scorpions
and crush them. Nothing will injure you. But don't rejoice
because evil spirits obey you; rejoice because your names are
registered in heaven.

—LUKE 10:19–20, NLT

When you tell a spirit to leave in Jesus's name, don't be surprised when you continue to deal with temptation, spiritual
attacks, or even supernatural phenomena. There are several key
points to remember. Jesus covers us with His authority, but we
are still called to stand firm in the battle. Sometimes this means
persevering through difficult circumstances. God never forsakes

us but helps us endure. We just have to remember to reach out to Him for strength and courage.

Do not fear the world, because God has already overcome it. When confronted by the enemy, be sure of your identity as a disciple of Christ. Believe that Jesus has all authority. Stand in the knowledge of God's grace. Serve God, blessing people in His name no matter how the enemy tries to get in your way.

Spiritual battles cause weariness to the spirit, mind, and body. Always rest in the loving embrace of God, who watches over you and never sleeps.

> My God, my rock, in whom I take refuge, my shield and the horn of my salvation, my stronghold and my refuge; my savior, You save me from violence.
> —2 SAMUEL 22:3, NAS

Digging Deeper

You then, my son, be strong in the grace that is in Christ
Jesus. And the things you have heard me say in the presence of many witnesses entrust to reliable men who will also
be qualified to teach others. Endure hardship with us like
a good soldier of Christ Jesus. No one serving as a soldier
gets involved in civilian affairs—he wants to please his commanding officer.

—2 Timothy 2:1–4

1. Are Christians afraid of spiritual warfare? Why?

2. Do you wear the armor of God?

3. What do you believe about spiritual warfare?

4. Do you know how to pray in the name of Jesus?

5. Have you been in a situation where you were called
   into spiritual battle? How did you respond?

A SPECIAL PRAYER FOR WARRIORS

My Lord,

Help me remember to put on the full armor every day. Protect my mind from temptation and wrong thinking. Guard my heart from acting on my desires rather than following the Holy Spirit. Remind me who I am in Christ Jesus, my identity as Your disciple and adopted child. When the fiery darts of the wicked one come against me, help me stand firm and to resist. Remind me of the truth every day. Write Your Word on my heart. Give me the strength to stand with my Christian brothers and sisters against the enemy.

In Jesus' s name, amen.

PART 4

THE EXTRA-SPECIAL STUFF

The heartfelt counsel of a friend is as sweet as perfume and incense.

< PROVERBS 27:9, NLT >

Chapter 28

YOU CAN KNOW JESUS— ASK ME HOW

I HAVE A VERY good friend. You could even say He's my *BFF* (best friend forever)!

He's the best guy you could ever hope to meet in the universe. He has a lot of names. You may even know some of them—Rabbi, Son of Man, the Word of God, the Good Shepherd, the Angel of God, Messiah, I AM, Wonderful Counselor, Prince of Peace, Alpha and Omega, Emmanuel (God with us), Savior, Lord.[1]

He is Jesus.

Do you know Him? I think Jesus is pretty special. But then He did save my life, my marriage, my—everything!

Have you spent time getting to know Jesus? I don't mean how religion portrays Him. Forget listening to what others say, the various "definitions" presented on cable channel specials dubiously titled *The REAL Jesus*. Everyone seems to have their own opinion or interpretation of who Jesus is, but do they know Him? Do they understand who He is?

His life. His death. His resurrection.

All the information floating around out there can be confusing. How can you know the true Jesus unless you meet Him? So please allow me to introduce you to my BFF. Well, let me point you in the right direction so you can figure it out for yourself.

The first step is to check out the first four books of the New Testament—the Gospels. Start with Matthew, and work your way through to John. You could probably read through them all in an afternoon.

I love the Gospels. These men knew Jesus. They are personal accounts of Jesus's life and ministry, recorded by witnesses (or disciples of witnesses) who had the major scoop. Learn how He ate with the lowest members of society, healed the sick, and set people free from demonic bondage with a word. Check out what Jesus had to say about life in Matthew 5–7. Pay attention to how He treated women and children. Are you surprised that Jesus had some choice words to shout at the religious establishment of the day?

When you've finished with the Gospels, read Isaiah 53 and Psalm 22 in the Old Testament. Those were written about Jesus too, hundreds of years before His humble birth in Bethlehem. In fact, there were over 360 prophecies written about the Messiah in the Old Testament. Jesus fulfilled them all!

But you have to read it for yourself.

You'll also find Jesus in the Book of Revelation—the end of the story, as it were. Now there is an eye-opener, let me tell you. Read it. The language can be tricky, so don't worry about the prophetic nature of the book right now. Try to see who Jesus is within the words—the Lamb of God.

Spending time in the Bible is really the only way to get to know God. Ask Him to show Himself to you, and He definitely will. God promises that anyone who seeks will find Him.

What can I say about how much I love Jesus?

He's always there with me, showing me a better way to treat my neighbor. He gives me strength when I'm weak, teaches me how to love. I am His disciple. He reminds me how He handles things. In truth, I haven't always been a great friend to Jesus. Some times I forget to call, or worse, do stuff I know would make Him shake His head. I turned my back on Him, getting all huffy when He didn't do things my way. But no matter what happens,

Jesus is always ready and waiting to forgive me and give me a hand up.

I've learned that being BFFs with the King of kings means you try to pattern your life after His.

So does any of this sound familiar? Is it new, or have you never really taken the time to pay attention? Maybe you are like I was and walked away from Jesus out of misplaced anger or spite. Friend, as long as you have breath in your body, it's never to late to turn around and say, "I'm sorry."

Do you know Jesus? If not, take a chance on finding out who He is for one simple reason—everything Jesus did before and after that cross *was for you*.

OK, I GET IT.
NOW WHAT DO I DO?

- *Admit*—Admit to God you are a sinner. Repent (agree with God) and turn away from your sins (Romans 3:23; 6:23; 1 John 1:9; Acts 3:19).

- *Believe*—Believe that Jesus is God's Son and that God sent Jesus to save people from their sins. Jesus died on the cross and rose from the dead (Romans 5:8; Acts 4:12; 16:31; John 3:16; 1 Peter 3:18; John 14:6).

- *Confess*—Tell Jesus you want Him to be the Lord of your life, and commit your life to Jesus. Trust Him to be your Savior (Romans 10:9–10, 13; Matthew 16:24; Luke 9:23).[2]

A SPECIAL PRAYER FOR SALVATION

Jesus,

I'm standing here in shock because I finally figured out who You are. You are the Savior. The one and only Son of God sent into the world because God loves me. The perfect sacrifice. Because of my sin You bled and died on a cross. I understand that it was the only way to make things right between You and me.

I'm overwhelmed by Your mercy. I can't believe You are giving me this freedom even though I don't deserve it. There is nothing I can do on my own to save myself. Your blood shed on the cross covers my sin. Only You can make me clean and whole.

Please be the Lord of my life. I want to serve You. I want every step to move forward with You and away from the person I was before. Show me how to be like You, Jesus. Thank You for Your love, God. I'm Yours.

In Jesus's name, amen.

If you made the choice to accept Jesus as your Savior—welcome! I'm so happy to have you as a brother or sister in Christ. Let me tell you, right now there is a party going on in heaven just for *YOU* (Luke 15:10)! And you may be wondering what to do next. Here are a few suggestions as you get started:

1. **Get a copy of the Bible.** Read it. Ask God to help you understand it. This is where you learn about Him, grace, and how to live. Learning God's way through Scripture is how we *renew our minds* (Romans 12:2).

2. **Find a local church with solid Bible teaching**. Say hello, get to know other Christians, and tell

them about your decision to follow Jesus. Ask someone to help you and show you the ropes. You are not walking the Christian life alone (Hebrews 10:25).

3. **Pray**. Talk to God. Remember, you don't have to be perfect. You will mess up (because we all do), so confess sin when it happens. Ask God to help you the next time temptation is in your way. Life as a Christian is about *freedom* (Galatians 5:1).

4. **Live what you believe**. You've made the commitment to Christ; now you want to reflect that in the decisions you make, the way you treat your family and others, and how you work on the job (John 14:23).

For more information about what comes next in your Christian life, you can call the Walking by Faith Prayer Line at 1-800-988-5120. Tell them you've just accepted Christ as your Savior. They will be happy to send you a free copy of *Your New Life* by Duane Vanderklok and pray with you.

Chapter 29

WHAT TO DO ABOUT YOGA?

HEN I WAS in seventh grade, my favorite television exercise program was *Lillias Yoga and You* on PBS.

The show aired in the afternoon. Every day after school, as soon as I got home, I'd rush up the stairs of our tri-level house to my bedroom. Books and papers were dumped on the bed. After changing into shorts and a T-shirt, I came flying back downstairs to turn on the TV and stretch with Lillias.

While practicing witchcraft, I began a daily yoga practice. One of the thirteen goals of a witch is to achieve spiritual, emotional, and physical balance. Staying healthy and getting fit was part of my spirituality. Yoga was the perfect avenue to work toward that achievement.

I bought a variety of DVDs, which I used for home practice. When I could afford the cost, I went to classes at a local yoga studio. I subscribed to popular yoga magazines. I embraced the American yoga culture.

When I rededicated my life to Christ, I continued my yoga practice. I knew there were religious and spiritual beliefs undergirding yoga, but I chose to ignore those in favor of the benefits. There is no denying regular yoga practice is great for general well-being and health. These days even doctors recommend yoga for stress relief and as therapy for heart patients.

I was fine until an article by Elliot Miller in the *Christian Research Journal* gave me pause to reconsider yoga's origins.[1]

The word *yoga* comes from the Sanskrit *yuj* meaning, "to yoke or join." The *Collins English Dictionary* defines *yoga* as: "a Hindu system of philosophy aiming at the mystical union of the self with the Supreme Being in a state of complete awareness and tranquility through certain physical and mental exercises."[2]

As a Christian I cannot deny the connection between Hinduism and yoga. Many will insist yoga as practiced today is little more than physical exercise. But I find it difficult to dismiss the original spiritual intent behind the asana, or various yoga postures.

However, I liked the feeling of accomplishment after my yoga practice. I enjoyed the physical challenge of performing a cobra or triangle pose. So I was faced with a dilemma—continue a daily exercise regimen of yoga, or find an alternative exercise. I hate to exercise. The idea of finding a decent replacement for yoga that would inspire consistency was not pleasant.

That's when I discovered "Christian" yoga.

My answer seemed clear. I could still practice yoga but overlay Christian meaning. I bought Christian yoga DVDs and attended several Christian yoga classes. The only problem was I was still hearing namaste ("I bow to the divine in you") at the beginning and end of class. I was still performing the traditional asana (Hatha yoga poses) and pranayama (restraining the prana or breath). I was being encouraged to meditate on a sacred word or think about the chakras (seven energy centers within the ethereal body).

Having repented of combining Christian beliefs with witchcraft, I found myself in a difficult position.

What was I going to do? I'm not a go-to-the-gym kind of gal. Walking is fine, but what was I going to do in the winter? I wanted a stretching exercise that provided stress relief. The answer came in a Christian alternative to yoga called "devotional exercise."

My first introduction came through PraiseMoves.[3] Laurette Willis had been involved in the New Age and practiced yoga for years before she became a Christian. Finding herself in a similar situation, she created a system of postures based on Scripture and letters of the Hebrew alphabet. She wanted to offer Christians an opportunity to achieve the benefits of low-impact, slow-movement exercise without compromising their spiritual beliefs. I love exercising with PraiseMoves DVDs. It's wonderful being able to focus my thoughts on the Lord as I move through each pose.

Another system of devotional exercise I practice daily and love was created by fitness expert Laura Monica. WholyFit offers exercise routines based on entire portions of Scripture.[4] My favorite is based on Ephesians 6:10–18. Talk about putting on the whole armor! You can meditate on God's Word, imprinting it on your heart, as you work through each posture. I use WholyFit DVDs, but classes are becoming available all over the country as Christians become aware of devotional exercise as a fitness alternative.

There are those within yoga or Christian yoga who don't see the difference between what they do and the devotional exercises provided through PraiseMoves or WholyFit. Are many of the poses similar? Definitely. There are only so many ways the body can move. Yoga doesn't hold any special claim on alignment or exercise postures that strengthen and tone muscles. What devotional exercise provides is an opportunity for a Christian to practice fitness and worship God through movement without compromise.

I can be healthy and fit (or moving toward that goal) while honoring God at the same time.

The subject of yoga (or Christian yoga) I found provokes very strong emotions in people. I think it's important to talk it through with gentleness and peace. I like Laura Monica's, founder of WholyFit, perspective: "There is no reason to condemn those who practice yoga. We can simply choose not to be part of the yoga culture."

Chapter 30

TIME FOR THE Q AND A

I HAVE THE PRIVILEGE of sharing my testimony by speaking at church, youth, and women's events. The most interesting (and challenging) part of these opportunities often arise during the question and answer portion of the meeting.

There is one thing these sessions have taught me. Christians are curious but uncomfortable talking about the supernatural, witchcraft, or paranormal with their church friends. Yet, when given the chance, many will pepper me with questions, eager to share their own experience or concerns.

So I decided to include a little Q and A in this book. The following questions (or similar variation) are those most commonly asked wherever I share my story.

"Are psychics and mediums evil? How is that possible when they give comfort to a grieving mother?"

I had finished speaking and answering questions at Unity Christian Music Festival 2010 when a woman approached me. She had lost her son to an accident the previous year. Although a Christian, she went to see a medium. The woman wanted to know if I thought psychics and mediums were evil.

My heart broke at the sorrow in her eyes.

Psychics and mediums are not evil people. Most have good hearts and desire to help others. The problem is that the source of their ability is not centered in God; therefore they don't see the truth. Spirits offering solace through the voice of a medium are liars. There is nothing benevolent about them. They are demons. It is in their nature to deceive. Mediums and psychics are convinced that what they are experiencing is good, light-filled, and from God. Their words are comforting, but the information they share is flawed. The medium is not interacting with a lost loved one but a demon in masquerade. The final outcome is confusion about God, faith, and salvation.

My question is—where were the Christians in this woman's life? Why did she feel compelled to go outside the church for comfort in a time of grief? This woman deserved the help of fellow Christians to bear her burden. She was apparently left alone. Such a thing should not happen. We are called to support and love one another as Christ loves us. It's what makes us the church.

"What's the problem with watching shows like *Ghost Hunters* or *Ghost Whisperer*?"

When it comes to ghost hunting, there are two important points Christians should keep in mind:

1. God condemns communication with the dead or seeking out people who do so:

When they say to you, "Consult the mediums and the spiritists who whisper and mutter," should not a people consult their God? Should they consult the dead on behalf of the living?
—ISAIAH 8:19, NAS

2. Spiritual deception:

For the time is coming when people will not endure sound teaching, but having itching ears they will accumulate for themselves teachers to suit their own passions, and will turn away from listening to the truth and wander off into myths.
—2 TIMOTHY 4:3–4, ESV

I believe ghost hunting is a risky activity and causes great harm, because it reinforces the belief that human spirits haunt or communicate with the living. Television programs such as *Ghost Hunters* and *Ghost Whisperer* promote that idea.

The Bible does not.

Sure, a mature Christian can watch those programs or movies without much harm to their faith. But what about the people around them? Will they take the time to discuss the important issues from a biblical perspective with family or friends? How about that new Christian who is still learning about God? Will they be able to discern between the information coming from the world as compared to Scripture? These are things we need to keep in mind. There are people watching us. They want to see if what we say matches what we do.

Paranormal reality shows or occult dramas promote a way of thinking I can't support.

I lived that life. Nothing good comes from feeding those interests.

"What do you think of Gettysburg? People claim to see ghosts of soldiers there. How can it not be real?"

I went to Gettysburg as a medium. The tragedy of the place overwhelmed me. Everywhere I went, I could see, hear, and feel the agony of the battle. The sensation of being lost was projected to me from "soldiers" throughout the area. In spiritual blindness I accepted the experience at face value.

I forgot who God is.

God is just. God is merciful. Would He allow human spirits to be stuck reenacting their deaths? Would He leave them, lost and alone, to their fate? Such an assertion suggests God has no power at all.

And those who believe God capable of such cruelty do not know Him.

Famous haunted locations such as Gettysburg, the Myrtles Plantation, or the Winchester Mansion are no different from private homes where paranormal activity is experienced. The source is the same. Scripture tells us demons have been roaming the world since ancient days. They appear in disguise to deceive. They are the source of all ghost or haunting activity in order to draw people into false beliefs about God.

"What is automatic writing?"

Automatic writing is a technique where the medium allows a spirit being to communicate through him or her by writing messages. The medium may be in a trance during the session. There are some mediums who practice automatic writing aware of everything but what their hand is writing.

What makes automatic writing dangerous is that a person gives control of his or her body to the spirit being during the process. There are some instances where a writer "hears a voice" and in essence takes dictation. In these cases the person is being used as a channel by a spirit being, but it's not true automatic writing.

Some confuse the concept of inspired writing with automatic writing. Being inspired while writing is not an occult activity. It should also not be confused with *God-breathed* writing, which is what we find in Scripture. The words recorded convey God's message, but the authors such as Paul, Peter, Isaiah, or Moses retained their distinct education, communication style, and personality. This is not the case in automatic writing.

Most people, when writing or being creative, are inspired by something. Yes, sometimes this can be spiritual but not necessarily demonic. God will inspire writers, musicians, and various other artists as they create in a variety of ways. The way to know the difference is the fruit of the labor. Does a poem, book, song, or movie have to be word for word from Scripture to be inspired by God? No, but it must agree with His written Word. Jesus should be acknowledged as Lord and Savior. This is how we can test and know what is from God.

"Can a Christian be psychic?"

Perhaps the question is: *Should* a Christian be a psychic? The obvious answer is no. A Christian who claims to be psychic or gifted by God as a psychic or medium is either not reading the Bible or ignoring what it says.

A psychic or medium communicates on a soul level with his or her guides and other spirit beings. God speaks to His people through gifts of prophecy, knowledge, and wisdom from the Holy Spirit to their spirit.

> Dear friends, do not believe everyone who claims to speak by the Spirit. You must test them to see if the spirit they have comes from God. For there are many false prophets in the world.
> —1 JOHN 4:1, NLT

"I can see auras. Isn't that a spiritual gift from God?"

I think it's important to understand what it means to "see" an aura. An aura is believed to be an energy field surrounding human beings that is invisible to the naked eye. It's believed a person's emotional or physical health can be discerned by the color, size, and strength of their aura. The aura can be perceived through inner eye or mind's eye awareness. When I was a witch and medium, I learned how to see auras. This activity was an integral part of occult practice designed to open my "third eye."

Auras and the ability to see them land squarely in the realm of the occult.

Some people will argue that seeing auras is similar to spiritual discernment. Discernment or discerning between spirits is listed in Scripture as a spiritual gift. However, the gift of discernment is the ability to know if a teaching is of God or is false. Discerning of spirits is knowing if a spirit is sent from God or not.

The ability to sense or detect auras has no connection with scriptural discernment.

I've heard people cite the examples of Moses's face "shining with light" from Exodus 34 or the transfiguration of Jesus on the mountain in Matthew 17 as a means of justifying purposeful viewing of auras.

In these passages the light surrounding Jesus or Moses is a reference to the physical presence of God's glory. These verses have nothing to do with visualizing a human aura.

The ability to see auras (and using the information) is not something we should seek out. And for those who seem able to detect auras naturally, I offer this word of caution: having a natural affinity does not suggest we should indulge in a practice or explore an ability—especially if it leads us into occult beliefs.

"Do you believe in demon possession (demonization)?"

Yes, but I believe it's unusual or rare. Those people who do experience true possession are more likely coming from an occult background or a religion such as Satanism or vodoun/voodoo. They are people who have never accepted or known Christ as Savior.

But I don't think that's who most Christians think of when they consider the question of possession. They are thinking of movies like *The Exorcist*. Maybe they are considering someone who is behaving oddly or telling strange stories. Perhaps they are concerned about themselves.

More often what is experienced is a form of *oppression*—a person being influenced through temptation by demonic spirits. There are also cases of spiritual harassment. This is not the same as being physically controlled by demons. I have a problem with people (or ministries) who blame the devil for everything. They give Satan much more power than he has, claiming possession even in professed Christians.

I believe many claims of possession or demonization are a

(unconscious) means of avoiding responsibility for one's own issues.

Scripture tells us when a person asks Jesus Christ to be Lord, that person is indwelt by the Holy Spirit. A person may have demons who follow or harass them because of former activities (especially occult related), but this should not be confused with possession.

"What do you think about Saul and the medium of Endor?"

I think people dwell too much on the part of the story about the medium conjuring Samuel, but I know they want my opinion as a former medium. So let's take a look at what happened in 1 Samuel 28.

The story of the medium of Endor is a cautionary tale about continued disobedience of God's commands. Saul was now rejected as king by God. Saul had an upcoming battle with the Philistines and wanted to know if God would give him a victory. God was not talking. No dreams. Nothing to the high priest through the Urim. The prophets were silent.

> So Saul disguised himself and put on other garments and went, he and two men with him. And they came to the woman by night. And he said, "Divine for me by a spirit and bring up for me whomever I shall name to you." The woman said to him, "Surely you know what Saul has done, how he has cut off the mediums and the necromancers from the land. Why then are you laying a trap for my life to bring about my death?" But Saul swore to her by the LORD, "As the LORD lives, no punishment shall come upon you for this thing."
>
> Then the woman said, "Whom shall I bring up for you?" He said, "Bring up Samuel for me." When the woman saw Samuel, she cried out with a loud voice. And the woman said to Saul, "Why have you deceived me? You are Saul." The king said to her, "Do not be afraid. What do you see?" And the woman said to Saul, "I see a god coming up out of the earth." He said to her, "What is his appearance?" And she said, "An

old man is coming up, and he is wrapped in a robe." And Saul
knew that it was Samuel, and he bowed with his face to the
ground and paid homage.

—1 SAMUEL 28:8–14, ESV

As a former medium I read the account as very similar to
what any medium might experience today. I think the spirit was
speaking through the woman to Saul. She was the one who saw
and described it. Was it truly Samuel? I don't know. Scripture
seems to indicate God allowed Samuel to be present. If this is the
case, it's one of those rare incidents where God worked through
the situation despite the circumstances. Not ideal, but effective. Perhaps it was a lying spirit meant to entice or deceive, as
recounted in 1 Kings 22:22. But the encounter with the medium
is not the point of the story. Saul's disobedience and the severe
consequence of his actions is the lesson to be learned.

A GLOSSARY OF OCCULT WORDS

air: One of the five magickal elements; represents sky, wind, high places, clouds, and east

adepts: People who are qualified (through sufficient study and practice) to accept and train an apprentice

Akashic record: A knowledge bank stored on the spiritual plane, said to have been in existence since the creation of the universe

altered state: A mental state that is different from normal waking (trance). Altered states can be achieved through Eastern meditation, hypnosis, and drug use.

amulet: An object (inscribed jewelry or stone) imbued with power to bind or repel bad luck, illness, curses

angel: A supernatural being; described in the Bible as "ministering spirits" of God

angelology: The systematic study of angels or beliefs about angels

Angel Oracle: A form of divination, similar to tarot, seeking angelic guidance

angel orb, orb: A solid or semitransparent ball of energy or light believed to be a spirit being. Orbs can be witnessed visually, in photographs, or on video camera footage.

apparition: The appearance of what is believed to be a human spirit as a ghost

apprentices: People in the process of learning witchcraft

Arcana, major: The twenty-two picture cards of the tarot. Each card depicts a scene featuring a person or several people and symbolic images.

Arcana, minor: The fifty-six cards of the tarot, often compared to modern playing cards. The cards are divided into four suits: wands/batons, cups, coins, and swords. The cards depict a symbolic scene and are number based.

Artemis: A goddess in Greek mythology. She was goddess of the hunt, wild animals, childbirth, and virginity.

asana: Individual exercise postures performed in yoga designed to control the body and unite mind/spirit to a supreme deity

astral body: A spirit body existing as part of the physical body, acting as a vehicle of the soul/consciousness

astral plane: A spiritual plane of existence

astral projection: Out-of-body experiences (OBEs) achieved through lucid or conscious dreaming, deep Eastern meditation, or the use of psychotropic drugs

astrology: A system that charts the relative position of stars and planets, interpreting information as it relates to human beings regarding personality, personal future decisions, global events, and so forth. Astrology should not be confused with astronomy (the scientific study of stars and planets).

athame: A knife used in Wiccan rituals for direction of power. Its use and purpose are strictly symbolic.

aura: Energy field emanating from the surface of a person or object. The energy can be visualized as an outline of color. The aura can be soul vibrations, the chakras, or a reflection of surrounding energy fields.

automatic writing: A process of writing in which the writer's conscious mind is not engaged. The activity can be done in a trance. Usually the writer is aware of hand movement but unaware of the content he or she is producing.

balefire: A fire used for ritual or magickal purposes; typically held outdoors (i.e., bonfire)

bane: Something that is evil, destructive, poisonous, or harmful

Beltane: April 30 through May 1 ("May Eve"); a fire festival recognizing the mating/marriage of the goddess and god; a celebration of the coming of summer

besom: A broom, usually constructed with twig, herb, or straw bristles on a stout wooden pole; used to *sweep away* negative energy

"Blessed be": A phrase used by witches and Wiccans as a wish for positive energy or blessings

bolline: A knife used to cut herbs for spell craft and Wiccan rituals

Book of Shadows: A private journal used in Wicca and witchcraft to write spells, keep ritual notes, record correspondences, deity information, sabbat information, express thoughts on the spiritual journey

Brighid: A goddess from Irish/Celtic mythology. She was a patroness of poetry, healing, and smith-work (the high arts). It is believed Brighid eventually became Saint Brigid after Ireland was converted to Christianity in mid-400s A.D.

Brujeria: Spanish folk magick

cauldron: A large, wide-mouthed metal kettle/pot. It is a symbol of rebirth in witchcraft and Wicca and represents the womb of the goddess. Depending on the size, it can be used in the sacred circle during ritual for burning incense or other objects.

chakra: The center of energy residing in the human body, aligned in an ascending column from the base of the spine to the top of the head

charge: An act of magick that infuses an object with a witch or Wiccan's personal power

channeling: Process of receiving messages, inspiration, and being used to communicate with them while possessed by spirit beings

charms: Objects that can be worn or carried that have been imbued with or are believed to hold magickal properties to bring luck, love, wealth, healing, protection, cursing, blessing, and so forth

clairalience: The ability to receive information through scents not otherwise discernible

clairambience: The ability to receive information through tastes not otherwise discernible

clairaudience: The ability to hear spirit voices not audible within normal hearing

claircognizance: The ability to know hidden information or knowledge

clairesentience: The ability to perceive spirit energy; the ability to receive hidden information or knowledge through physical sensations in the body

clairvoyance: The ability to perceive or "see" hidden information or knowledge through visions

corn dolly: A human figure created from twisting and plaiting stalks of grain, representing fertility

coven: A group of witches or Wiccans who meet for sabbat celebrations, rituals, and spell craft. Initiation is usually required.

crone: A Wiccan deity; the aspect of the Triple Goddess representing wisdom and maturity

crystal glass/ball: Used to aid clairvoyance and in a technique known as *scrying*. Images are seen in crystals or other mediums such as water and are interpreted.

demon: A supernatural being described as a malevolent spirit; a fallen angel rebelling against God

demonology: The systematic study of demons or beliefs about demons

deosil: A clockwise turn

devil: Title given to the supernatural being who acts as tempter of humankind. The devil commands a force of lesser evil spirits known as demons. He is a fallen archangel of God: aka Lucifer, Satan, the serpent, the great dragon.

divination: Divination is the process of using tools, methods, or symbols to determine or foretell the future

dowsing: A method of divination using a pair of rods to find water, iron ores, missing objects, direction

earth: One of the five magickal elements; represents caves, mountains, groves, plains, and north

Eastern meditation: A practice designed to create an altered state of consciousness, freeing the practitioner to experience spiritual unity with a supreme deity

ecstatic dance: Free form movement inspired by music designed to release or express strong emotion

ectoplasm: A term coined by Charles Richet meant to describe a substance created by physical mediums while in a trance state; also considered a physical manifestation of ghosts and what enables psychokinesis (movement of objects with the mind) to occur

elements: Earth, air, fire, and water—the four substances considered to be the building blocks of the universe

elemental spirit: Mythical beings associated with the four elements: gnomes (earth), sylphs (air), nymphs (water), and salamanders (fire). Faeries are also associated with elemental spirits.

EMF: Electromagnetic field

empath: A person who possesses the ability to feel the emotions of other beings

entity: A spirit being

Esbat: A full-moon ritual

esoteric: Doctrines or practices of obscure, specialized, enlightened, or secret knowledge

ESP: Extra sensory perception involves awareness of information not gained through normal senses and not deducible from previous experience. Classic forms of ESP include telepathy, clairvoyance, and precognition.

ethereal plane: The vital, life-sustaining force of living beings and the vital energy in all natural processes of the universe; a New Age/theosophic belief.

ethereal body: A New Age term for the life force/aura. It's considered the blueprint of the physical body. The ethereal body (or aura) is used for diagnosis and treatment in energy healing techniques such as Reiki.

evil: Objectionable behavior/thought that is excessively hateful, cruel, or violent; devoid of moral/ethical conscience

evil eye: A look believed to cause bad luck, a curse, or injury

evocation: The calling up of spirits for visible or invisible visitation

EVP: Electronic Voice Phenomenon

familiar: A spirit that aids a witch embodied in an animal such as a cat; a demon that empowers a witch, psychic, or medium

fertility ritual: Religious ritual that reenacts (physically or symbolically) sexual acts leading to reproduction

fire: One of the five magickal elements; represents deserts, volcanoes, lightning, sun, stars, and south

folk magick: A system of magick using natural elements such as herbs, stones, and the power of the practitioner in spell craft

ghost: Believed to be the non-corporeal manifestation of the spirit or soul of a dead person that has remained on earth after death

ghost hunt: An amateur paranormal investigation performed by a ghost hunter attempting to prove or disprove a haunting. Equipment used may include an EMF (electromagnetic field) detector, video cameras, digital cameras, recorders, and thermometers, infrared, full spectrum illumination, motion detectors, and so forth.

ghost hunter: A person who uses pseudoscientific methods to research the existence of ghosts; an amateur investigator

goblets: A metal or glass drinking cup with a stem and foot Goblets can be used in rituals for drinking wine or other beverages, as a symbol of the womb in fertility rituals, and the like.

grimoire: A book of magick (example: *The Key of Solomon*, sixteenth to seventeenth century)

guardian spirit: A spirit that protects and guides an individual person

handfasting: A pagan or Wiccan wedding

Hatha: A system of yoga introduced by a fifteenth-century yogi named Swatmarama

haunting: A spirit or ghost that manifests through apparition and/or unexplained activity such as footsteps, opening/closing doors, moving objects, whispers, knocks, bangs, and so forth

hereditary witch: A person born into witchcraft or who has innate magickal ability

horoscope: A chart of the sun, moon, and planets with their significant astrological aspects in regard to a special date, such as a person's birthday or major event

hypnosis: An altered state of consciousness that leaves people open to outside suggestion or direction

hypnotherapy: The use of hypnosis for therapeutic treatment

Imbolc: February 2 (Candlemas); a fire festival commemorating Brighid, looking toward spring as the goddess recovers from giving birth to the god (Yule)

incorporeal: A spiritual state without a body or substance

intuition: A form of immediate knowledge

intuitive: A person who is sensitive to the subtle energies of people and things around them

invocation: The act of calling upon or petitioning a deity or spirit; an act of prayer

jinn: A pre-Islamic spirit lower than an angel with power to influence humans for good or evil (genie)

Karma: The effects of all deeds past, present, and future, whether good or bad

kirtan: A form of Hindu meditation involving chanted singing in call and response form

kundalini: A type of energy found in Hindu belief described as a serpent coiled at the base of the spine

Lammas/Lughnasadh: August 1; a fire festival commemorating the first harvest/fruits; also symbolizes the weakening of the god as days grow shorter

levitation: To rise or float in the air through supernatural means in defiance of gravity

Mabon: September 21 (autumn equinox); a festival celebrating the second harvest and preparing for winter

Maiden: A Wiccan deity; an aspect of the Triple Goddess representing virginity

magick: An activity performed in the mundane world that intersects with the spirit realm to create physical change through intention

manifestation: The materialized form of a spirit

manifesting: An action brought to reality through force of spirit or will

Mantra: A sound, word, or phrase repeated in succession during meditation. A mantra is designed to foster a state of relaxation and alter mental/spiritual awareness.

Mary Worth: The main character of an urban legend and divination/conjuring game known as *Bloody Mary*. There are many stories about Mary's origins. Some myths say she was a beautiful girl who was murdered; others implicate Mary as the killer. The game consists of standing before a mirror in a dark room (typically a bathroom) staring into the mirror while chanting "Mary Worth" or "I believe in Mary Worth." The point of the game is to see the reflection of Mary standing behind you or Mary's face instead of your own.

medium: A person with the ability to communicate with the dead or other spirit beings

"Merry meet": A phrase used by witches and Wiccans as a form of good will and greeting

"Merry part": A phrase used by witches and Wiccans to bestow good will upon leaving

metaphysics: Philosophy concerned with explaining the nature of reality beyond the physical world

Midsummer: June 21 (summer solstice, Litha); a festival commemorating the sun and the god at the height of power

mist column: An unexplained column of mist that appears in a photo or on video but is not visibly present in the environment

Mother/Mother Goddess: A Wiccan deity; an aspect of the Triple Goddess representing fertility

mysticism: Spiritual practices with the intent of achieving direct experience with the divine

namaste: A Hindu/Sanskrit greeting that translates, "The god/goddess/spirit within me greets/recognizes/honors the god/goddess/spirit within you."

near-death experience: A near-death experience (NDE) is an experience reported by a person who has experienced clinical death and was revived. Dr. Raymond Moody is credited with increasing interest in NDE (a term he coined) through his book *Life After Life* (Mockingbird Books, 1975).

neopagan: A person who follows Wicca (contemporary paganism)

numerology: A system of divining the mystical relationship between numbers and important dates or events

occult: Secret or hidden knowledge

old ones: A Wiccan reference to the ancient gods and goddesses

om: A vibration/sound used as a mantra for chanting

open circle: A ritual that is open for participation by people outside of a specific coven

open ritual circle: A ritual that is for participation by people outside of a specific coven and/or open to the general public for observation and/or participation

oracle: A person, place, or shrine where revelation can be sought from a pagan deity

Ostara: March 21 (spring equinox); a festival celebrating the beginning of true spring, the fertility of the goddess, and the return of the sun after winter

Ouija board: A game that uses a board and planchette for the express purpose of spirit communication

out-of-body experience: An out-of-body experience (OBE) involves a sensation of floating above or traveling outside of the body.

pagan: A person who follows polytheistic religion

paganism: Any religion that includes ritual, worship, and devotion to multiple deities

pantheons: All the gods/goddesses of a specific people or religion

paranormal: Phenomena that appear or are created outside of natural occurrences

paranormal activity: A situation in which unexplained phenomena are occurring

parapsychology: The scientific study of paranormal phenomena

past-life regression: A hypnosis therapy technique used to induce memories of past lives

pendulum: A weight suspended from a fixed point that can swing freely; example—a quartz stone pendant on a necklace chain

portal: A doorway or entrance between the physical and spiritual worlds

polarity: The concept of equal but opposite spiritual energy

pranayama: A Sanskrit word meaning "restraint of breath"; slow, controlled breathing

premonition: A vision, sensation, or experience of future events

prophecy: The prediction of future events or speaking of divine words through human messengers (prophets)

psychic: A person who possesses extrasensory abilities, including clairvoyance, psychometry, and precognition. A psychic medium can also communicate with spirits.

psychotropic herbs or plants: Marijuana, calamus, peyote, and other herbs/plants that can be used to create an altered state of consciousness

reading: A consultation with a psychic or medium that is meant to provide insight and guidance, communication with spirit beings, and the like

reincarnation: The belief that a living spirit is reborn into a new form over many lifetimes. Traditional reincarnation allows anything from a bug to human. Western reincarnation emphasizes human to human rebirth.

remote viewing: The gathering of psychic information while the object of the reading is hidden from physical perception by location or distance

ritual: A ceremony performed for symbolic emotional, spiritual, or religious value

routes: pathways

runes: Pictographs/figures based on Germanic alphabets from the third to thirteenth centuries (example: Old Norse); typically imprinted on stones for divination. They can also be inscribed for use in spell craft.

sacred circle: A space marked out for ritual. The circle may be drawn on the ground, marked by branches or string, or drawn in chalk. The circle can be created through visualization of energy, forming sacred space. A circle provides protection during spell casting.

salt: Recognized by world cultures as a means to absorb or bind spiritual energy; used for protection, purification, and healing

Samhain: October 31; a fire festival marking the death of the god to await rebirth; a time of remembrance

Satanism (The Church of Satan): A humanistic religion that uses Satan as a symbol in ritual, created in the 1960s by Anton LaVey

scrying: A method of future-casting (divining) through gazing at a crystal, bowl of water, blackened mirror, or other reflective surface inducing visions

séance: A meeting of people attempting to communicate with the dead through a medium

seekers: People with a desire to be trained in traditional witchcraft

self-styled Satanist: An individual religious expression or belief in Satan as a deity that is on the fringe or independent of the traditional Church of Satan or Theistic Satanist teaching.

shadow self: The darker emotions/side of human personality (anger, greed, fear, etc.)

simple feast: A ritual meal shared with the god and goddess (example: cakes and ale)

skyclad: A Wiccan term for nudity that occurs in a ritual

spell: Directed intention to bend universal energy for a desired outcome

spell craft: The spiritual art of magick

solitary: A witch or Wiccan who practices the Craft alone

spirit: One of the five magickal elements; it encompasses the energy of the other four, connecting them together.

spirit board: A hand-crafted device used to communicate with spirit beings; another name for the Ouija board

spirit communication: An ability/activity allowing the living to communicate with spirit beings; another term for mediumship or channeling

spirit guide: A term used by mediums and psychics to describe an entity that acts as a spiritual counsel or protector to a living human being. The term can also refer to animals, totems, angels, or nature spirits.

spiritism: The belief in the survival of human souls after death and the importance of communication with them

spiritualism: A religious movement that began in the United States and was prominent in the 1840s to 1920s, especially in English-speaking countries. The movement's distinguishing feature is a belief that the spirits of the dead can communicate through mediums.

spirituality: Focusing on personal experience and understanding self in relationship to the universe

spiritual energy: A metaphorical term often used to describe a variety of unexplained phenomena, psychic experience, universal life force, spirit life force, etc.

spiritual healing: A method of self-empowerment or self-actualization process seeking the meaning of life; an unexplained physical healing of the body

Stregheria: Italian folk magick

supernatural: Forces or phenomena not observed in nature and beyond verifiable measurement

syncretism: the blending of different religions or schools of thought into a unified whole

talisman: An object (inscribed jewelry or stone) imbued with power to draw luck, love, good fortune, health

tarot: A system of divination using a deck of seventy-eight cards, divided into Major and Minor Arcana, with allegorical symbols on each card, which the reader uses to "read" the past, present, and future

telepathy: Communication from one mind to another by a means other than the perceptual senses

Theistic Satanism (also known as Traditional or Spiritual Satanism): A religion worshipping Satan as a deity through ritual. Spell casting may be employed depending on the beliefs of the practitioner. Theistic Satanists worship Satan as a deity.

The Craft: A reference to witchcraft, folk magick, and Wicca

The Great Rite: A symbolic act of intimate union between the goddess and the god reenacted by a Wiccan high priest and priestess during the ritual circle as the high priest plunges an athame into a chalice held by the high priestess.

The Triple Goddess: A Wiccan deity; the female half of a duotheistic system. She is represented as "the Maiden, the Mother, and the Crone." She represents the stages of a woman's life, the phases of the moon, and so forth.

triquetra: A Celtic knot symbol for trinity; represents the Triple Goddess in Wicca and witchcraft

The Horned God: A Wiccan deity; the male half of a duotheistic system; the consort of the Triple Goddess

totem: Any entity watching over a family, clan, or tribe; mostly associated with native religious beliefs

trance: An altered state of consciousness different from a normal waking state

tradition: Typically a structured Wiccan subgroup with unique ritual practices

vigil: A process during a ghost hunt in which the ghost hunter and/or medium attempts to illicit a response from the haunting spirit; a kind of séance

visualization: Forming pictures in the mind's eye for use in magick

voodoo/vodoun: A religion syncretizing animism, magick, and Catholic tradition; ritual revolves around a large pantheon of West African deities, deified ancestors, and saints

voodoo doll: A human-shaped charm imbued with power for luck or cursing

vortex: Believed to be a method of transport for spirits between the spirit and physical worlds

wands: A stick or rod used during spell casting

warlock: An old English term for male witch meaning "deceiver." It is considered to be derogatory and is not used by serious modern practitioners.

water: One of the five magickal elements; represents lakes, wells, rivers, oceans, tides, and west

water witching: A form of dowsing using thin rods or a thin, forked stick to detect the subtle energy or presence of natural substances such as minerals, ores, metal objects, water, etc.

Wheel of the Year: The cycle of holiday's followed by Wiccans, pagans, and witches known as sabbats. Four occur on the solstices and equinoxes (quarter days): Midwinter/Yule, Ostara, Midsummer/Litha, and Autumn/Mabon. The other four are midway between them (cross-quarter): Samhain, Imbolc, Beltane, and Lammas/Lughnasadh. The quarter days are based on Germanic traditions, and the cross-quarter days are based on Celtic fire festivals.

white light: visualized positive spiritual energy

white noise: A steady sound or electronic noise with a wide range of frequencies

Wicca: An earth-centric, duotheistic pagan religion founded by Gerald Gardner in the 1950s. Wiccans worship the goddess and the god through a variety of ancient pantheons, incorporating reenvisioned pagan ritual and magick.

Wiccan: A person who practices the religion of Wicca

widdershins: A counter-clockwise turn

witch: A person who lives with a magickal worldview, is an ally with nature, and expresses his or her spiritual identity through witchcraft

witchcraft: A worldview, spiritual art, and spiritual path that relies on the use of spell craft and nature; harnessing personal and universal energy to accomplish individual goals or desires

witch blood: An intuitive knowledge or understanding of witchcraft

witch path: A term used to describe witchcraft as a personal, spiritual belief

Yin/Yang: Two primal opposing but complementary cosmic forces. The concept is the cornerstone of Taoism and traditional Chinese medicine.

yoga: A system of physical exercises designed to focus mind and spirit into unity with a supreme deity

Yule: December 21 (winter solstice); a festival commemorating the rebirth of the god from the goddess; a celebration of life and light during the harshness of winter

MY GHOST-HUNTING DAYS

A picture taken in 2005. I'm wearing a triquetra (Celtic trinity knot) necklace, symbolizing my spiritual identity as a Christian witch. All the jewelry I wore as a witch and medium had double meaning. The earrings corresponded with inner peace and balance.

My quartz crystal pendent necklace doubled as a pendulum during investigations. I'm attempting communication while my teammate monitors EMF readings. Renters claiming to have experienced haunt activities abandoned the house during renovations.

The bridge where I told a negative spirit it had to stay on the other side. I believed the two orbs (light spheres) in the picture (a large one above my forehead and small one in front of me) were the energy of my spirit guide, Michael.

Waiting for the team to finish packing up at the end of the bridge investigation.

Sharing my "impressions" of spiritual energy from a
grave marker while investigating a cemetery.

My final ghost hunt in November 2007. My teammate and
I are inspecting an area where the EMF detector had been
lighting up in answer to questions moments before.

Appendix C

My 2009 Mission Trip to Costa Rica

Vans transported us around the city of Palmares between host homes, mission work sites, and the host church.

Costa Rica is a beautiful country with friendly people. They smile, whatever their circumstances in life.

I loved the exotic plants and animals. Tropical fruit
trees grew in everyone's front courtyard.

Going on a prayer walk through the neighborhoods near our host
church. The day was hot, water was off throughout the city.

Our teams did work projects the entire week. My work project team went to a local orphanage. We cleaned, sorted clothes, and painted the courtyard fence. We also spent time hanging out with the children.

The local custom is to stand at the gate and call out
a greeting to whoever is in the house.

We spent time walking through Palmares on Sunday after morning worship. There was a beautiful historic Catholic church.

For our final day in Costa Rica our hosts took us sightseeing. We visited Baldi Hot Springs, located at the base of Arenal Volcano in La Fortuna, San Carlos. Yes, that is smoke billowing from the top.

A NOTE FROM KRISTINE

ESCAPING THE CAULDRON is an informative memoir about my personal journey into the occult. The information shared is from memory and experience. I have purposefully chosen not to include occult resource information. The last thing I want is to send you, dear friend, down the wrong path.

Instead, here are additional resources you can use to learn more about the occult from a biblical perspective:

Christian websites:

- equip.org
- gotquestions.org
- christiananswers.net
- biblegateway.com
- christiananswersforthenewage.org

Christian books

- *Dancing With the Devil*, Jeff Harshbarger, editor (Charisma House, 2012)
- *Wicca's Charm*, Catherine Edwards Sanders (Shaw Books, 2005)
- *What's the Deal With Wicca?*, Steve Russo (Bethany House, 2005)
- *The Truth Behind Ghosts, Mediums, and Psychic Phenomena*, Ron Rhodes (Harvest House, 2006)
- *The Ouija Board: A Doorway to the Occult*, Edmond C. Gruss (P & R, 1994)

NOTES

CHAPTER 7
EASTERN MEDITATION: GATEWAY TO THE OCCULT

1. See GotQuestions.org, "What Is Soaking Prayer?", http://www
.gotquestions.org/soaking-prayer.html (accessed May 2, 2012).

2. Two websites with additional information about Christian meditation that you may want to review are: Waylon B. Moore, "Bible Meditation: An Unexpected Source of Success for Christians,"
MentoringDisciples.org, http://www.mentoring-disciples.org/
Meditation.html (accessed May 2, 2012); and Mary Askew, "What Do
You Do After Doing a Bible Study?", http://www.explorecareersand
collegemajors.com/meditate_on_Word_of_God.html (accessed May 2,
2012).

CHAPTER 8
DIVINATION AND FAMILIAR SPIRITS

1. Angelfire.com, "Familiar Spirits, Divination, Witch, Medium and
Necromancer," http://www.angelfire.com/in/HisName/familiar.html
(accessed May 2, 2012).

CHAPTER 10
PURSUING THE PARANORMAL

1. David W. Moore, "Three in Four Americans Believe in Paranormal," Gallup.com, June 16, 2005, http://www.gallup.com/
poll/16915/three-four-americans-believe-paranormal.aspx (accessed
May 3, 2012).

2. Robert Roy Britt, "People Said to Believe in Aliens and Ghosts
More Than God," LiveScience.com, November 24, 2008, http://www
.livescience.com/7608-people-aliens-ghosts-god.html (accessed May 3,
2012).

3. See also Sue Bohlin, "Was Reincarnation Ever in the Bible?",
Probe Ministries, http://www.probe.org/site/c.fdKEIMNsEoG/
b.4222727/k.4FCD/Was_Reincarnation_Ever_in_the_Bible.htm
(accessed May 3, 2012).

Chapter 11
Spirits: Angels and Demons

1. ChristianAnswers.net, "What Does the Bible Teach About Angels?", http://www.christiananswers.net/q-acb/acb-t005.html#1%20%28angels%29 (accessed May 3, 2012).

2. C. S. Lewis, *The Screwtape Letters* (New York: Harper Collins, 2001), ix.

Chapter 12
Origins of a Ghost Hunter

1. *Merriam-Webster's Collegiate Dictionary*, 11th ed. (Springfield, MA: Merriam-Webster, Inc., 2003), s.v. "conjure."

Chapter 13
Dangerous Games

1. Will Wright, "Behind the Magic 8 Ball—a History of America's Favorite Fortune Teller," Yahoo! Voices, October 18, 2007, http://voices.yahoo.com/behind-magic-8-ball-history-americas-favorite-603478.html (accessed May 3, 2012).

2. Bill Ellis, *Lucifer Ascending: The Occult in Folklore and Popular Culture* (Lexington, KY: The University Press of Kentucky, 2004), 163–169.

3. Samuel Pepys, *The Diary of Samuel Pepys* (n.p.: Modern Library, 2001), 159.

Chapter 15
Mediums and Psychics

1. Belinda Elliott, "Do You Believe in Ghosts?", CBN.com, http://www.cbn.com/entertainment/books/elliott_ghosts.aspx (accessed May 3, 2012).

Chapter 20
How Should Christians Respond?

1. Josh Kimball, "Wicca Experts Encourage Christians to Engage America's 'Fastest-Growing' Religion," ChristianPost.com, September 21, 2008, http://www.christianpost.com/news/wicca-experts-encourage-christians-to-engage-america-s-fastest-growing-religion-34408/ (accessed May 3, 2012).

CHAPTER 21
SPIRITUAL GIFTS

1. For more information about spiritual gifts, see David Holt Boshart Jr., "Gifts of the Holy Spirit," ChristCenteredMall.com, http://www.christcenteredmall.com/teachings/gifts/index.htm (accessed May 3, 2012).

CHAPTER 22
THE DANGERS OF DABBLING

1. Dictionary.com, *Dictionary.com Unabridged* (New York: Random House, Inc., n.d.), s.v. "dabble," http://dictionary.reference.com/browse/dabble (accessed May 4, 2012).

CHAPTER 24
THE TWILIGHT SAGA

1. Sue Bohlin, "The Darkness of Twilight," Probe Ministries, http://www.probe.org/site/c.fdKEIMNsEoG/b.6099193/k.76B1/The_Darkness_of_Twilight.htm (accessed May 4, 2012).

CHAPTER 26
THE ORIGINS OF HALLOWEEN

1. For more background information on Halloween, there are several very good resources you may want to check. They include: Kristine McGuire, "The Origins of Halloween," and other blog entries at *Kristine ReMixed*, accessed at: kristinemcguire.com; "Christians and Halloween," GracetoYou.org, http://www.gty.org/Resources/Articles/1126 (accessed May 4, 2012); and Hank Hanegraaff, "Halloween for Christians: Oppression or Opportunity," Christian Research Institute, http://www.equip.org/articles/halloween-for-christians-oppression-or-opportunity (accessed May 4, 2012).

CHAPTER 28
YOU CAN KNOW JESUS—ASK ME HOW

1. Herbert Lockyer, compiler, "The Names of Jesus," Tentmaker.org, http://www.tentmaker.org/lists/names.html (accessed May 4, 2012).

2. *Pentecostal Evangel*, "The ABCs of Salvation," http://pe.ag.org/Salvation.cfm (accessed August 29, 2011).

CHAPTER 29
WHAT TO DO ABOUT YOGA?

1. Elliott Miller, "The Yoga Boom: A Call for Christian Discernment," *Christian Research Journal* 31, no. 2 (November 2, 2008).

2. *Collins English Dictionary*, complete and unabridged 10th ed. (New York: HarperCollins Publisher, n.d.), s.v. "yoga," Dictionary.com, http://dictionary.reference.com/browse/yoga (accessed May 1, 2012).

3. Laurette Willis, "Why a Christian Alternative to Yoga?", PraiseMoves.com, http://praisemoves.com/about-us/why-a-christian -alternative-to-yoga/ (accessed May 4, 2012).

4. For more information about WholyFit, visit their website at www .wholyfit.org.